What's Become of Australian Cultural Studies?

Cultural studies face a complicated yet rich future, proving both flexible and resilient in many countries. Against this backdrop, this book offers a fresh perspective on the state of the field of cultural studies, via an evaluation of the work of one of its key thinkers – Graeme Turner – and the traditions of Australian cultural studies which have been influential on the formation of the field.

Thinking with Turner, and being informed by his practice, can help orient us in the face of new challenges and contexts across culture, media, and everyday life; teaching and pedagogy; the relation of research to the new politics of public engagement, policy, management, and universities; the internationalization of cultural studies and the reconfiguration of nationalism; the changing concepts and relations of culture; the development of important new areas in cultural studies, such as celebrity studies; and the emergence of digital media studies.

This lively and provocative volume is essential reading for anyone interested in where cultural studies has come from, where it's heading to, and what kinds of ideas – not least from Graeme Turner – will help scholars and students alike make sense of and reconfigure the discipline.

This book was originally published as a special issue of *Cultural Studies*.

Gerard Goggin is Professor of Media and Communications and ARC Future Fellow at the University of Sydney, Australia.

Anna Cristina Pertierra is Senior Lecturer in Cultural and Social Analysis at the University of Western Sydney, Australia.

Mark Andrejevic is Professor in the Department of Media Studies, Pomona College, Claremont, CA, USA.

Melissa Gregg is Principal Engineer in User Experience Research at Intel labs, based in Portland, OR, USA.

What's Become of Australian Cultural Studies?

The legacies of Graeme Turner

Edited by
**Gerard Goggin, Anna Cristina Pertierra,
Mark Andrejevic and Melissa Gregg**

Routledge
Taylor & Francis Group

LONDON AND NEW YORK

First published 2017 by Routledge

2 Park Square, Milton Park, Abingdon, Oxfordshire OX14 4RN
52 Vanderbilt Avenue, New York, NY 10017

Routledge is an imprint of the Taylor & Francis Group, an informa business

First issued in paperback 2018

British Library Cataloguing in Publication Data
A catalogue record for this book is available from the British Library

ISBN 13: 978-1-138-68488-1 (hbk)
ISBN 13: 978-0-367-19143-6 (pbk)

Typeset in Perpetua
by RefineCatch Limited, Bungay, Suffolk

Publisher's Note
The publisher accepts responsibility for any inconsistencies that may have
arisen during the conversion of this book from journal articles to book chapters,
namely the possible inclusion of journal terminology.

Disclaimer
Every effort has been made to contact copyright holders for their permission to
reprint material in this book. The publishers would be grateful to hear from any
copyright holder who is not here acknowledged and will undertake to rectify
any errors or omissions in future editions of this book.

Contents

Citation Information

The chapters in this book were originally published in *Cultural Studies*, volume 29, issue 4 (July 2015). When citing this material, please use the original page numbering for each article, as follows:

Chapter 1
What's become of Australian cultural studies: The legacies of Graeme Turner
Gerard Goggin, Anna Pertierra and Mark Andrejevic
Cultural Studies, volume 29, issue 4 (July 2015), pp. 491–502

Chapter 2
Turning up to play: 'GT' and the modern game
Meaghan Morris
Cultural Studies, volume 29, issue 4 (July 2015), pp. 503–514

Chapter 3
Dependencia *meets gentle nationalism*
Toby Miller
Cultural Studies, volume 29, issue 4 (July 2015), pp. 515–526

Chapter 4
Kylie will be OK: On the (im-)possibility of Australian celebrity studies
Frances Bonner
Cultural Studies, volume 29, issue 4 (July 2015), pp. 527–545

Chapter 5
Cultural studies and the culture concept
Tony Bennett
Cultural Studies, volume 29, issue 4 (July 2015), pp. 546–568

Chapter 6
Politics as scholarly practice: Graeme Turner and the art of advocacy
John C. Byron
Cultural Studies, volume 29, issue 4 (July 2015), pp. 569–589

Chapter 7

The effective academic executive
Melissa Gregg
Cultural Studies, volume 29, issue 4 (July 2015), pp. 590–608

Chapter 8

Afterword: So ... what has become of Australian cultural studies?
Graeme Turner
Cultural Studies, volume 29, issue 4 (July 2015), pp. 609–614

For any permission-related enquiries please visit:
http://www.tandfonline.com/page/help/permissions

Notes on Contributors

Mark Andrejevic is Professor in the Department of Media Studies, Pomona College, Claremont, CA, USA.

Tony Bennett is Research Professor in Social and Cultural Theory in the Institute for Culture and Society at the University of Western Sydney, Australia. He is a member of the Australian Academy of the Humanities and of the Academy of the Social Sciences in the UK. His main books include *Formalism and Marxism* (1979), *Bond and Beyond: The Political Career of a Popular Hero* (1987, with Janet Woollacott), *Outside Literature* (1991), *The Birth of the Museum* (1995), *Culture: A Reformer's Science* (1998), *Pasts Beyond Memory: Evolution, Museums, Colonialism* (2004), and *Making Culture, Changing Society* (2013). He is also a co-author of *Accounting for Tastes: Australian Everyday Cultures* (1999) and *Culture, Class, Distinction* (2009).

Frances Bonner is an Honorary Research Associate Professor in Television and Popular Culture in the English, Media Studies and Art History School at the University of Queensland, Australia. Her research focuses on non-fiction television, celebrity, magazines and most recently, adaptation. In addition to many articles and chapters on these topics, she is the author of *Personality Presenters* (2011), *Ordinary Television* (2003), and co-author, with Graeme Turner and David Marshall, of *Fame Games: The Production of Celebrity in Australia* (2000).

John C. Byron has worked in Australian higher education and research policy and administration for over 15 years. He was Executive Director of the AAH from August 2003 to May 2010. He has also been Senior Adviser to Senator the Hon Kim Carr, Australian Minister for Innovation, Industry, Science and Research and Minister for Higher Education, Dean of Research and Graduate Studies in the Faculty of Humanities at Curtin University, and President of the Council of Australian Postgraduate Associations. He has taught at the universities of Sydney (English) and Wollongong (Creative Writing). He has served on numerous institutional, sector and government advisory, management and selection boards, and is currently on the Sydney University Press Advisory Board. He has a first-class honours degree and a university medal from the University of Adelaide and a PhD from the University of Sydney, both in English Literature. He is an Honorary Fellow of the University of Melbourne's Centre for the Study of Higher Education.

Gerard Goggin is Professor of Media and Communications and ARC Future Fellow at the University of Sydney, Australia.

Melissa Gregg is a Principal Engineer at Intel Corporation studying the future of work. Her publications include *Work's Intimacy* (2011), *The Affect Theory Reader* (co-edited with Gregory J. Seigworth, 2010), and the forthcoming *Counterproductive*. Before joining Intel, Melissa was a faculty member in the Department of Gender and Cultural Studies at the University of Sydney (2009–2013) following successive postdoctoral fellowships at the Centre for Critical and Cultural Studies, University of Queensland (2004–2008).

Toby Miller is a Professor of Journalism, Media and Cultural Studies at Cardiff University/Prifysgol Caerdydd, Sir Walter Murdoch Professor of Cultural Policy Studies at Murdoch University, and Profesor Invitado at the Universidad del Norte. He lives in London.

Meaghan Morris is Professor of Gender and Cultural Studies at the University of Sydney, Distinguished Adjunct Professor at Lingnan University, Hong Kong, and Chair of the Inter-Asia Cultural Studies Society. Formerly Chair Professor of Cultural Studies at Lingnan (2000–2012), she writes on the rhetoric of nationality in transnational conditions, and her books include *Too Soon, Too Late: History in Popular Culture* (1998), *Hong Kong Connections: Transnational Imagination in Action Cinema* (co-edited with Siu-leung Li and Stephen Chan Ching-kiu, 2005); *Identity Anecdotes: Translation and Media Culture* (2006), and *Creativity and Academic Activism: Instituting Cultural Studies* (co-edited with Mette Hjort, 2012).

Anna Pertierra is Senior Lecturer in Cultural and Social Analysis at the University of Western Sydney, Australia.

Graeme Turner is Emeritus Professor in Cultural Studies at the University of Queensland, Australia. His most recent publications include (with Anna Pertierra) *Locating Television* (Routledge, 2013), and *Reinventing the Media* (Routledge, 2015).

Gerard Goggin, Anna Pertierra and Mark Andrejevic

WHAT'S BECOME OF AUSTRALIAN CULTURAL STUDIES

The legacies of Graeme Turner

This article introduces the special issue of Cultural Studies *commemorating and evaluating the contribution of Graeme Turner to the field. This article provides a brief introduction to Turner, his key ideas and what resources they offer for cultural studies today and into the future. In particular, we suggest that Turner's work and legacies needs are bound up with the trajectories of Australian cultural studies — and its place and circulation in international cultural studies.*

Cultural studies scholars find themselves in an extremely interesting and complicated moment. Displacing its anglophone originary myths, the field of cultural studies has fast internationalized (Abbas and Erni 2005). Despite its anti-disciplinarity skew, it has proven a resilient and flexible formation in many countries. Taken as synonymous with the fatuities of postmodernism — often the byword in public discourse for the decline of the civilized humanities — cultural studies has flourished as a de facto bridge across humanities specializations. Decried for its vacuous theoretical predilections, the rise in cultural research's fortune has seen the discipline forge productive, powerful collaborations with public, private and governmental organizations, and in some countries, even figure in national research policy and priorities. Resilient, even celebratory (in an appropriately sceptical manner) in surmounting these mixed fortunes, cultural studies in the 2010s faces profound challenges and complex new opportunities — that arise from the new politics of culture, everyday life, social experience and power relations. Recurrent questions have been discussed of how, why, for what purpose, where and with whom should cultural studies be advanced? (Grossberg 2010). Cultural studies has always developed with the accompanying strains of its attendant critical self-assessment. In this, one of the leading figures, a trenchant critical intelligence and honest broker, remains Professor Graeme Turner.

1

Turner's work as a leading scholar of media and cultural studies is well known internationally. His clear voice and deft synthesis have made cultural studies penetrable to the undergraduate novice without ever losing the attention of his contemporaries. But what might be less well known to those who have never worked alongside Turner is that his excellence in areas beyond research and publication has been equally important to the formation of cultural studies as a distinctive discipline within Australia. As a mentor, his ideas and advice have influenced new generations of Australian scholars. As a manager, he has demonstrated ways in which this skill, usually detested by humanities academics, can actually improve the working lives of those around him. As a lobbyist, he has represented the humanities to universities and governments across Australia, with great effect.

This collection of papers aims to capture and reflect upon these broader dimensions of Turner's work and the importance of these dynamics of mentoring, management and institutionalization (Morris and Hjorth 2012, Striphas 1998), as well as specific national and regional conditions, policy and politics for the forms cultural studies takes. The anthology was inspired by an event that was held at the University of Queensland in Brisbane, Australia, in August 2012 to mark Turner's retirement. Turner retired from his official position at the University of Queensland in 2012 but remains very active as a researcher, mentor and humanities policy adviser. The commemorative event held at the University of Queensland reflected not only on Turner's substantial record as a scholar but also on the building of Australian cultural studies more generally. Turner's career, blending the ideas, politics and practices of building a new field of study, was representative of many of the qualities that make cultural studies in Australia distinctive. Building on this event, this special issue takes the opportunity of Turner's (non-)retirement to consider the legacies of his work and the project of Australian cultural studies in general – and what these now signify for cultural studies.

The four of us who initiated this project – the three of us, plus Melissa Gregg, who was influential in its early phase – met through our time at Turner's peerless Centre for Critical and Cultural Studies (with the telltale abbreviation CCCS). While the CCCS was frequently referred to as 'Graeme's Centre', it is a testament to Turner's approach to fostering research that he himself saw the intellectual productivity of the CCCS as resulting from collaborative mutual support among the resident scholars, while the burdens of securing funding and maintaining political goodwill on behalf of 'his' Centre remained his alone. Our idea was that through a critical re-evaluation of Turner's writings, teaching, policy and advocacy, this special issue could also contribute towards the much needed accounting under way of the possibilities, politics, prospects and programmes for advancing cultural studies into the coming decades. This is an endeavour which Turner catalysed with his trenchant *What's Become of Cultural Studies* (Turner 2012), and to which other distinguished cultural studies figures have contributed. Thus we hope that this collection of papers would serve not only to reflect upon the impact of Turner's work as an individual but also to consider how Australian cultural studies has made contributions to global discussions of media and culture – and what directions and possibilities the antipodean angle offers now.

About Graeme Turner

Born in Sydney on 2 September 1947, Turner took a BA (Hons) in literature at the University of Sydney (1965–1968), then travelled to Canada for his MA (Hons) at Queen's University, Kingston, Ontario, awarded in 1970. Returning to Australia, from 1971 to 1973, Turner taught at Mitchell College of Advanced Education, in Bathurst, a regional city three hours' drive from Sydney. He returned overseas to study for a Ph.D. in the School of English and American Studies, University of East Anglia, UK, which was awarded in 1977.

Back in Australia, Turner moved to Perth, Western Australia, to teach in the School of English at the Western Australian Institute of Technology, where the humanities were being shaken up by the new ideas in cultural, film and media studies. Here Turner was a key figure in various projects that proved decisive for the formation of a distinctively Australian cultural studies. During the time Turner was there, Perth was home to figures such as John Fiske (Fiske *et al.* 1987), with whom he collaborated on book projects, as well as other significant figures in the field such as John Hartley and Toby Miller (see Miller's contribution here – Miller 2015; on this period, see also Frow 2007 and King and Turner 2010).

Turner moved to Queensland in 1985 to take up a Senior Lectureship at the Queensland Institute of Technology (which became Queensland University of Technology). In 1989, he moved across town to the University of Queensland to take up an Associate Professorship in the Department of English, assuming a full professorship in 1994. After serving as Head of School, in 1999, with strong support from the Vice Chancellor, he established the CCCS, where post-retirement he continues as Emeritus Professor. Other important relationships with Australia-based cultural studies scholars would flourish in this period – with those in Brisbane such as Stuart Cunningham, Tony Bennett and John Frow (who also moved from Perth to Brisbane to work at the University of Queensland), and also with those circulating through Sydney, such as Meaghan Morris (see Morris 2015), Ien Ang (who also migrated from Perth to the East Coast, founding the Centre for Cultural Research at University of Western Sydney), Elspeth Probyn (after she moved from Canada to properly establish cultural studies at the University of Sydney), and many others.

Through his long, productive and canny career, Turner has contributed to a number of fields but characteristically always with cultural studies as an abiding presence and decisive base. Turner established himself as an important theorist of cinema and film studies (Turner 1988, 2002). He was a pioneer in cultural studies approaches to studying national culture, through his many publications on Australian culture, media and society (Turner 1986, 1993, 1994, Kuna and Turner 1994). A rock musician himself, Turner has made important contributions to contemporary music research (Bennett *et al.* 1993). Turner is a key figure in television studies, co-author and co-editor of important collections and books. Initially focusing on Australian television (Tulloch and Turner 1989, Turner and Cunningham 2000), Turner became increasingly preoccupied with how to achieve an adequate, genuinely international understanding of contemporary television in its new digital, post-broadcast ecologies (Pertierra and Turner 2013, Sinclair and Turner 2004, Tay *et al.* 2015; Turner and Tay 2009, 2010). Turner was one of the early movers in celebrity studies (Turner *et al.* 2000, Turner 2004), which has proven a rich vein of enquiry to provide a critical way into interrogating developments in media and culture such as the turn to reality television, user-generated content, digital platforms and other instances of the 'demotic turn' in media and culture (Turner 2010). Elsewhere over many years, Turner has maintained a critical stance and engagement with news, current affairs, talk radio and journalism (Turner 1996, 2005, Turner and Crofts 2007).

Through this wide-ranging intellectual endeavour, Turner has been a consistent mainstay of Australian cultural studies. In turn, Australian cultural studies has been an important force in the international development of cultural studies as a discipline – something represented by the career of the pioneering journal *Australian Journal of Cultural Studies*, which commenced and was published in Perth (from 1983 to 1987), then was expatriated from 1987 to the present day as *Cultural Studies* (Frow 2007, Morris 1992).

Alongside his own research on film, television and national culture, Turner established his claims to speak of cultural studies, through his widely read 1990 *British Cultural Studies: An Introduction* (Turner 1990). As well as providing one of the first systematic accounts of British cultural studies, one was one of the first textbooks in the discipline generally. For Turner himself, it provided an explicit way to work out his own position on, claim to, and, advice for, cultural studies, something he addressed explicitly in the famous 1990 *Cultural Studies Now and in the Future* conference held at the University of Illinois at Urbana-Champaign (see Turner 1992a, Turner *et al.* 1992).

In the early 1990s, especially, there was a nominative and institutionalizing conjuncture for Australian cultural studies, marked by various important discussions of what this might constitute and do (for instance see Ang, 1992, Ang and Hartley 1992, Benterrak *et al.* 1984, Frow and Morris 1993, Muecke 1992). Turner was a consistent theorist of the relationship of Australian cultural studies and the generativeness and limits of its *specificity*, as he often put it, against the typical reluctance of gradually internationalizing cultural studies to explicitly locate its various parts (see, for instance, Turner 1992b, Grossberg 1993).

This emphasis on the need to locate cultural studies has been an important, continuing thread in Turner's work up to his latest work on international television, supported by a prestigious Australian Research Council (ARC) Federation Fellowship. The material support for Turner for undertaking large-scale empirical and theoretical work brought together in this *Locating Television* project was also very much provided by the CCCS.

He built the CCCS into a world-class research centre, especially through his appointment and nurturing of steady flow of talented postdoctoral researchers – something for which he became renowned (see Gregg 2015, in this volume). During this time, he employed 21 researchers on full-time positions: Mark Andrejevic, Melissa Bellanta, Gerard Goggin, Ben Goldsmith, Melissa Gregg, Ramaswami Harindranath, Anita Harris, Gay Hawkins, Sukhmani Khorana, Geert Lovink, Abigail Loxham, Carmen Luke, Mark McLelland, Adrian Mabbott Athique, Anna Pertierra, Morgan Richards, Graham St John, Jinna Tay, Anthea Taylor, Zala Volcic and Kitty van Vuuren. Most of these researchers commenced as postdoctoral fellows, and their time at CCCS proved pivotal to their flourishing as fully fledged scholars pursuing academic careers.

The CCCS was the base for a very significant initiative that leveraged Turner's expertise in mentoring, and greatly fertilized the field, especially through systematically and creatively bringing together Australia's abundance of distinguished cultural studies scholars, with the next generations. This was the Cultural Research Network (CRN; 2004–2009), a national group of top cultural researchers, funded by the ARC, that Turner initiated and led. Genuinely interdisciplinary between cultural studies and adjoining disciplines, including cultural history, cultural geography and cultural anthropology, CRN provided a matrix for stimulating, developing and theorizing a wide range of international visits and exchanges, minor and major projects, many of which have resulted in important studies, contributions to policy and practice, funded projects and major publications.

At the same time as directing CCCS, Turner took on a powerful national role as a voice for the humanities sector – eventually as an influential president of the Australian Academy of Humanities, developing national research policy (e.g. Turner 2008), directly advocating and negotiating with successive education ministers, and earning a place on the Prime Minister's Science, Innovation and Engineering Council (discussed here by Byron 2015).

These are the lineaments of Turner's work, career, style and engagements that deserve to be taken together for reassessment; not just for a *Festschrift*, rather for the models, concepts, strategies, practical value and resources they offer for thinking about what might become of cultural studies – the pretext of this special issue.

Circulating Australian cultural studies: Graeme Turner's legacies

The six papers that responded to this invitation, each provide a perspective on Turner's legacies and what they portend for larger questions and tendencies in national and international cultural studies.

Meaghan Morris kicks off with a reprise of her unforgettable tribute to Turner at his August 2012 Brisbane send-off. Morris situates Turner's emergence within the flows and contra-flows of cultural studies currents in Australia in the 1980s and 1990s. She characterizes his formative key contribution in this period as being able to:

> 'multiply' Australian hypotheses about national identity by combining a critique of the public uses of nationalism by business heroes pursuing private gain with a positive vision of the democratic and diversifying potential of the media and the public cultural institutions.

Morris points out that Turner continues his fascination with the national, in the subsequent period – as of now – when the national is unmade, and remade, and emphasizes his ability, as he shifts gears into policy and advocacy work, to construct new ideas for the national. Among other things, Morris evokes the remarkable investment and importance Turner accorded teaching, in his version of cultural studies, especially through the popularity, clarity and longevity of his many textbooks.

Toby Miller offers an expansive, global account of Turner's work. Like Morris, he is drawn to the centrality of the national in Turner's work which he suggestively terms 'gentle nationalism'. Drawing from the theoretical and political traditions of the global south, especially from the ideas of Latin American intellectuals, Miller uses the concept of *dependencia* to stipulate the precise sense in which Turner comes from the margins – and in doing so draws our awareness, once more, to the core-periphery, colonial relations, that Australian and other forms of cultural studies straddle, take energies from, adapt and refuse. As he unfolds his account, Miller offers an especially helpful overview and characterization of the Australian higher education system, and where it fits internationally – something indispensable for situating Turner's ideas, practices and effects.

Frances Bonner takes up such concerns from a different tack, focusing on the fascinating case of celebrity studies. Here Turner's work, with hers, David Marshall, and other Australian-based scholars, such as Sean Redmond, has directly led the formation of the area of celebrity studies. She notes that Turner has been especially concerned to sheet home the more celebratory, textualist accounts of celebrity to treatments of the industry, economy, format, forms and social functions of celebrity. Bonner's assessment, however, gives pause. She suggests that one:

of the problems posed for an analysis of the state of Australian celebrity studies is that so many of its researchers, most notably Turner, Marshall and Redmond, are leading international scholars in the field. They publish internationally and speak generally about celebrity, never disavowing their location, but only occasionally mentioning matters specifically related to Australia. Even when they do, the point is rarely to talk of national concerns.

This is the fortunate fall of many Australian cultural studies scholars, especially those of us who work on areas – digital technologies and media, for instance – that translate more easily into the circuits of international, global north, academe and publishing. The issue that remains, however, is the uncertain future for work that wishes – or needs to – remain located, or repatriated, as Bonner observes in relation to celebrity studies:

> In conjunction with the publishing changes which have led to fewer local monographs and more scholars publishing internationally on internationally recognisable celebrities, the existence of Australian celebrity studies cannot be regarded as secure.

For Bonner, the implications of these changes are not clear-cut, but at the least she finds that 'integration of celebrity into a broader analysis of Australian culture that characterised the earlier period is certainly less evident' (Bonner 2015).

With Tony Bennett, we return to the question of national in Turner's work, but reframed from the most fundamental question in cultural studies: how do we understand culture? Bennett notes the lack of considered attention given to culture as a 'way of life' in cultural studies, despite the common reflex among many scholars to regard this as the discipline's authorizing concept. Bennett seeks to complicate the genealogies of culture as a concept, by detailed examination of the 'conceptual prehistories' of cultural studies, in particular the American anthropological tradition. In contrast to Turner, and much of Australian cultural studies, borrowing and definition against Britain, Bennett considers the US example important for showing 'the processes involved in adjusting an imported concept of culture to the task of shaping a national culture that was to be defined against the elitist credentials of European humanist culture'. Bennett argues that 'the American history of the culture concept also speaks directly to the roles that culture has played in Australia's post-war trajectories' (Bennett 2015).

John Byron offers a compelling account of Turner as national policy advocate, with his forceful and definitive work as President of the Australian Academy of the Humanities. Byron offers us important insights into the relationships among politics, policy and scholarship practice that have been a constitutive feature of various strands of Australian cultural studies, and that it turned out Turner was especially well placed to finesse. Byron provides the paper of record on this chapter in Australian cultural studies, at the apogee of the discipline's claim to represent the humanities. Byron's account is very much rooted in the Australian context, yet nicely contextualized – with many lessons and resonances for cultural studies, across different national and regional settings.

Melissa Gregg, alumna of Turner's CCCS, grasps the nettle of acknowledging, situating and theorizing his work of management. Noting the reluctance of cultural studies to abide, let alone, credit management, Gregg develops a rich account of the conceptual, strategic, affective, collaborative and bureaucratic work that goes into good cultural studies work-as-management – for which she argues Turner is a truly representative exemplar. As Gregg argues:

> As a field, we are challenged by Graeme's legacy to work together to influence the terms of our own management, especially so that no one individual carries the responsibility for the field and its forward momentum … Adhoc professionals turn to each other for support to withstand the turbulent conditions of work in the knowledge industries, to find methods for succeeding in spite of them. We may not all seek to be executives, but collectively we can be effective.

Turner himself has the last word, in this issue at least. He notes the changed institutional configurations of cultural studies in Australian universities, as the peculiar neoliberal policies have sharpened up. In his view, cultural studies research has built an impressive base in Australia in the 2000s marked by productive interdisciplinary collaborations and strong international participation of leading researchers. The new locations of this research have shifted, with Asia being key, generating 'still rich and effective ways of performing the located-ness of Australian cultural studies'. For Turner, this leaves cultural nationalism as a less likely or necessary position for orienting an intellectual position or career, even if important topics for national politics and audiences still require attention. Finally, Turner returns to teaching, where he sees cultural studies in undergraduate programme as having the opportunity to retain its earlier energy, appeal and relevance.

We are grateful to all six contributors for their excellent papers and willingness to take up the challenge of reflecting on Graeme Turner's body of work – and through this, the trajectories of cultural studies viewed via its antipodean skews. We also wish to thank the reviewers, for the difficult task of commenting on the distinctive papers that such a commemorative anthology generates. There are many issues raised by the special issue that we hope will serve as resources for wider issues and debates in cultural studies internationally. For our part, we wished to close by remarking on just two threads in this conversation.

We note the focus on questions of power relations and their critique, which remain a constant in Turner's work – a fact that continues to position him in relation to developments in the field. If the academic politics surrounding the development of Cultural Studies programmes has sometimes been figured in terms of the academic status of cultural forms, Turner has kept his eye on the underlying social issues this development was meant to serve. In the face of the academic shorthand that all too quickly figures a flipping of the binaries as politically subversive (as if the gesture of gate-crashing the ivory tower by swapping Shakespeare for *The Sopranos* amounted to sociopolitical empower-ment), Turner has kept his eye on the underlying 'structures of domination' to which '[w]ork in cultural studies has consistently addressed itself' (1990, p. 5) and has always been canny enough to recognize that the desire to '*épater la bourgeoisie*' is simply another of the bourgeoisie's own diversions. The point has never been to study popular culture as if were 'high culture' (and thereby to tweak the sophisticates), but to recast the study of culture (mass, popular and otherwise) in ways that excavate its social and political functions: to interrogate not just the culture but the society that produced it. This understanding has underwritten both the excitement and energy Turner brought to the development of cultural studies in the Australian context and his concerns regarding subsequent developments that have laid claim to its mantle despite 'surrendering the core political objectives of cultural studies' (2012, p. 178). If the academic politics that once resisted the development of the field have transformed significantly, the broader political and societal concerns that cultural studies sought to address remain with us. This persistence contributes to the enduring relevance of the version of cultural studies Turner crafted (and continues to develop).

Finally, across the day's activities in August 2012 which marked Turner's official retirement and inspired this collection of papers, there was a recurring observation of Graeme Turner's working style which we believe is unusual and special even among the very esteemed colleagues with whom he shares the claim to have pioneered the field of Cultural Studies. That is that he puts into everyday practice as a colleague the values of openness, transparency, collaboration and propensity to pleasure which are often held to be valued in the abstract of cultural studies but are not always so easily manifested in the corridors and staff meetings of real-life academia. This particularly valuable quality of Turner's is perhaps best appreciated 'from below', by those who have worked under him as a Director and mentor. Not only has Turner always been available for consultation, advice, encouragement or the occasional critique, but also he assures junior colleagues that he finds such exchanges genuinely rewarding. It is precisely this attitude that, we hope, has modelled some future directions for new generations of cultural studies scholars both within Australia and beyond.

Disclosure statement

No potential conflict of interest was reported by the authors.

References

Abbas, A. & Erni, J., eds. (2005) *Internationalizing Cultural Studies: An Anthology*, Malden, MA, Blackwell.

Ang, I. (1992) 'Dismantling "Cultural Studies"?', *Cultural Studies*, vol. 6, no. 3, pp. 311–321.

Ang, I. & Hartley, J., eds. (1992) '"Dismantle Fremantle"/Dismantling "Cultural Studies"?', special issue of *Cultural Studies*, vol. 6, no. 3.

Bennett, T. (2015) 'Cultural Studies and the culture concept', *Cultural Studies*. doi:10.1080/09502386.2014.1000605.

Bennett, T., *et al.*, eds. (1993) *Rock and Popular Music: Politics, Policies, Institutions*, London and New York, Routledge.

Benterrak, K., Muecke, S. & Roe, P. (1984) *Reading the Country: An Introduction to Nomadology*, Fremantle, WA, Fremantle Arts Centre Press.

Bonner, F. (2015) 'Kylie will be OK: On the (im-)possibility of Australian Celebrity Studies', *Cultural Studies*. doi:10.1080/09502386.2014.1000606.

Byron, J. (2015) 'Politics as scholarly practice: Graeme Turner and the art of advocacy', *Cultural Studies*. doi:10.1080/09502386.2014.1000607.

Fiske, J., Hodge, B. & Turner, G. (1987) *Myths of Oz: Reading Australian Popular Culture*, Sydney, Allen & Unwin.

Frow, J. (2007) 'Australian Cultural Studies: theory, story, history', *Postcolonial Studies*, vol. 10, no. 1, pp. 59–75.

Frow, J. & Morris, M. (1993) 'Introduction', in *Australian Cultural Studies: A Reader*, ed. J. Frow & M. Morrs, Sydney, Allen & Uwin, and Urbana, IL, University of Illinois Press, pp. vii–xxxii.

Gregg, M. (2015) 'The effective academic executive', *Cultural Studies*. doi:10.1080/09502386.2014.1000609.

Grossberg, L. (1993) 'Cultural Studies and/in new worlds', *Critical Studies in Mass Communication*, vol. 10, no. 1, pp. 1–22.

Grossberg, L. (2010) *Cultural Studies in the Future Tense*, Durham, NC, Duke University Press.

King, N. & Turner G. (2010) 'Interview with Professor Graeme Turner, University of Queensland, November 9, 2007', *Television & New Media*, vol. 11, no. 2, pp. 143–156.

Kuna, F. & Turner, G., ed. (1994) *Studying Australian Culture: An Introduction*, Hamburg, Verlag Dr. Kovač.

Miller, T. (2015) 'Dependencia meets gentle nationalism', *Cultural Studies*. doi:10.1080/09502386.2014.1000610.

Morris, M. (1992) 'Afterthoughts on "Australianism"', *Cultural Studies*, vol. 6, no. 3, pp. 468–475.

Morris, M. (2015) 'Turning up to play: "GT" and the modern game', *Cultural Studies*. doi:10.1080/09502386.2014.1000611.

Morris, M. & Hjorth, M., eds. (2012) *Creativity and Academic Activism: Instituting Cultural Studies*, Durham, NC, Duke University Press, and Hong Kong, Hong Kong University Press.

Muecke, S. (1992) *Textual Spaces: Aboriginality and Cultural Studies*, Sydney, UNSW Press.

Pertierra, A. & Turner, G. (2013) *Locating Television: Zones of Consumption*, London and New York, Routledge.

Sinclair, J. & Turner, G., eds. (2004) *Contemporary World Television*. London, BFI.

Striphas, T., ed. (1998) 'Special issue on "The Institutionalization of Cultural Studies"', *Cultural Studies*, vol. 12, no. 4.

Tay, J., Iwabuchi, K. & Turner, G., eds. (2015) *Television Histories in Asia*, New York, Routledge.

Tay, J. & Turner, G. (2010) 'Not the apocalypse: television futures in the digital age', *International Journal of Digital Television*, vol. 1, no. 1, pp. 31–50.

Tulloch, J. & Turner, G., eds. (1989) *Australian Television: Programs, Pleasures and Politics*, Sydney, London, Boston and Wellington, Allen & Unwin.

Turner, G. (1986) *National Fictions: Literature, Film, and the Construction of Australian Narrative*, Sydney, London, and Boston, MA, Allen & Unwin.

Turner, G. (1988) *Film as Social Practice*, 1st edn, London and New York, Routledge.

Turner, G. (1990) *British Cultural Studies*, 1st edn, Boston, MA, London, and Sydney, Unwin Hyman.

Turner, G. (1992a) '"It works for me": British Cultural Studies, Australian Cultural Studies, Australian Film', in *Cultural Studies*, ed. L. Grossberg, C. Nelson & P. Treichler, New York, Routledge, pp. 640–649.

Turner G. (1992b) 'Of rocks and hard places: the colonized, the national and Australian Cultural Studies', *Cultural Studies*, vol. 6, no. 3, pp. 424–432.

Turner, G., ed. (1993) *Nation, Culture, Text: Australian Cultural and Media Studies*, London, Routledge.

Turner, G. (1994) *Making It National: Nationalism and Australian Popular Culture*, Sydney, Allen & Unwin.

Turner, G. (1996) *Literature, Journalism and the Media, Foundation for Australian Literary Studies*, Townsville, James Cook University.

Turner, G., ed. (2002) *Film Cultures Reader*, London, Routledge.

Turner, G. (2004) *Understanding Celebrity*, London, Sage.

Turner, G. (2005) *Ending the Affair: The Decline of Television Current Affairs in Australia,* Sydney, University of New South Wales Press.

Turner, G. (2008) *Towards an Australian Humanities Digital Archive*, Canberra, Australian Academy of the Humanities, http://www.humanities.org.au/Portals/0/documents/Policy/Research/Towards_An_Australian_Digital_Humanities_Archive.pdf (accessed 16 October 2014).

Turner, G. (2010) *Ordinary Media and the Media: The Demotic Turn*, Los Angeles, CA, Sage.

Turner, G. (2012) *What's Become of Cultural Studies*, London, Sage.

Turner, G., *et al.* (1992) '"Discussion" of "It Works for Me": British Cultural Studies, Australian Cultural Studies, Australian Film', in *Cultural Studies*, ed. L. Grossberg, C. Nelson & P. Treichler, New York, Routledge, pp. 650–653.

Turner, G., Bonner, F. & Marshall, P. (2000) *Fame Games: The Production of Celebrity in Australia*, Cambridge and New York, Cambridge University Press.

Turner, G. & Crofts, S. (2007) 'Jonestalk: the specificity of Alan Jones', *Media International Australia*, no. 122, pp. 132–149.

Turner, G. & Cunningham, S., eds. (2000) *The Australian TV Book*, Sydney, Allen & Unwin.

Turner, G. & Tay, J., eds. (2009) *Television Studies after TV: Understanding Television in the Post-Broadcast Era*, London and New York, Routledge.

Meaghan Morris

TURNING UP TO PLAY

'GT' and the modern game

Reviewing the 'all-round' nature of Graeme Turner's academic practice and its impact on the development of Cultural Studies in Australia since the 1980s, this introductory article explores the relationship between Turner's institutional effectiveness and the mode of creativity fostered by the game of Rugby League.

On 31 August 2012, a capacity crowd turned up to the University of Queensland for a symposium on 'Building Australian Cultural Studies: the work of Graeme Turner'. Many of the speakers assembled to honour the legend widely known around Australia as 'GT' had worked in Brisbane with Graeme through one of his crowning achievements as an institution-builder, the UQ Centre for Critical and Cultural Studies that was hosting the event. It was my task to kick off and, as a blow-in from Sydney (one of many from other cities in attendance that day), I felt unusually nervous in front of GT's home crowd – given some of the memories I might have drawn on in my speech.

Graeme Turner and I did not spend our youth building Australian Cultural Studies together. Passing the 1980s on opposite sides of the continent, we did not even meet in Australia. Our first encounter was a hit-up in print over feminism, populism and national culture following the publication of *Myths of Oz* (Fiske, Hodge and Turner 1988).[1] When we finally occupied the same space-time continuum for the 1990 'Cultural Studies Now and in the Future' conference at Urbana-Champaign in the USA (Grossberg *et al.* 1992), our mutual friends expected to see a bit of biff.[2] So, I daresay, did we: Graeme had just written an introduction to *British Cultural Studies* (Turner 1990) while I had published a polemic about 'Banality in Cultural Studies' (Morris 1990b) that took a good swipe at both Baudrillard and the British. Yet we got on like a house on fire, sharing then and to this day a chemical consensus about what matters, what's important about academic work and how you go about doing it.

As I came to know Graeme better I realized that our shared love of Rugby League explains something of this chemistry. GT is probably the only scholar I know who would offer me tickets for a Brisbane Broncos game that clashed with his farewell party. He is certainly the only one for whom I would turn those tickets down.

As the legendary commentator, coach and former player Phil Gould remarks on a more or less weekly basis, 'it's a funny game, Rugby League' (Chesterton 1996; Gould 2013). Like all great games, League is a philosophy of life. In all forms of rugby you progress by directing energy (throwing the ball) backwards or sideways while charging and dodging numerous large, threatening obstacles coming at you full-tilt from all sides. However, one of the harsh particularities of the modern game of League is that the set of tackles in possession is limited to five. It's a hard, grinding game that requires immense reserves of stamina, patience, finesse, parochial fire and single-minded ferocity of purpose to avoid obliteration, sustain momentum and, occasionally, score – self-evidently (it seems to me) a great preparation for creative life in the Australian academy. Parochial energy can be a resource for pulling off the impossible in institutions as it is in Rugby League (Morris 2005, p. 23). While we are well past the time when one's town or state of origin forever circumscribed belonging, unalterably grounding identity, the capacity to *care* ferociously about the place and community for which you are trying to make space is a force for innovation in any social contest. This capacity marks the difference between a legend and a star or celebrity player who arcs through a world of fame. Sonny Bill Williams is a star but Wally Lewis is a legend.[3] Legends serve the people; they are loved and remembered for the lasting gifts their struggles bring to others. Undoubtedly a star in several academic fields, not least celebrity studies (Turner 2004), Graeme Turner is a legend in this sense.

In recognition of this, the Symposium organizer Gay Hawkins asked us to reflect on the collective achievements of Cultural Studies in Australia over the decades co-extensive with Graeme Turner's career. So let me look backwards to ask what has changed in the big picture since we had that early collision over *Myths of Oz*. I think it's fair to say that at the time this circulated as a stoush between 'Australian feminist criticism' (me) and 'blokey Anglo-Australian Cultural Studies' (Graeme). In retrospect, much more solid themes that would dominate the field for the next 20 years are manifest in Graeme's response to his critics, 'Return to Oz' (Turner 1991). There he discussed the relationship between academic knowledges and popular audiences; the pedagogic function of academic books written accessibly for students and general readers; how to create a version of Australian Studies founded on the multiplicities of cultural meanings active across the nation rather than on the pursuit of a mythic 'essential core' of identity; and the role of government reports and professional infrastructure initiatives (associations, conferences) in shaping a discipline's future. The importance of the latter in particular was not widely appreciated at the time and 'Return to Oz' reads now as a visionary document. However, what also strikes me forcibly is how *pre*-national most of us were in the 1980s. Accessible air travel across Australia was still a relative novelty and our networks, our thinking and our practices were primarily regional in the sub-national sense.

Certainly, on the West Coast academics based in Perth were editing an innovative national journal. Founded in 1983, the *Australian Journal of Cultural Studies* (*AJCS*, the precursor to *Cultural Studies*) included Graeme, John Fiske and John Frow on its editorial board and drew contributions from what now looks like a stellar line-up from across the country (Tony Bennett, Stuart Cunningham, John Hartley, Sylvia Lawson and Tom O'Regan, among others).[4] Yet for me on the 'East Coast' – a generous construal of links between handfuls of people mostly based in Sydney and Melbourne – the activities of *AJCS* were remote. Still a free-lance journalist and part-time teacher in 1983, I bought *AJCS* because I collected 'little magazines' in the old literary manner. I do not remember reading it back then. My intellectual networks arose from the social movements of the 1970s (Anti-Psychiatry, Gay Liberation, Residents'Action and Women's Liberation); from Communist Party reading groups; and from the self-organizing world of anarchist pub debate that had thrived for many decades in Sydney. Elements of these fed into the lively public culture surrounding the 1970s Australian film revival (Murray 1980, Hodsdon 2001) and then the 'art world' fever of the 1980s (Sangster 1987, Foss 2009). In those days I felt sorry for people who were 'only academics' and did not pay their writing much attention.

Writing about this period in our discipline's history, John Frow (2005) points out that intellectual 'clusters' that seem highly visible now were always transient and marked as much by disconnection as by overlap or intersection; people whose work seems to 'belong' together historically were barely aware of each other's existence. In retrospect the most cosmopolitan Australian cities of the 1980s were probably Adelaide (the Arts Festival capital) and Brisbane, where young scholars from the bigger cities were washing up in the first significant post-war wave of academic labour migrancy. While international events provided a platform for Sydney or Perth people to become 'Australian' together elsewhere, a disconnection in theoretical and political orientation meant that those who were involved with British Cultural Studies did not travel the same routes as we who followed French and Italian debates directly in those languages – that is, not until 'Cultural Studies Now and in the Future' made a bridge of the US academy that not only enabled new trans-Australian encounters to take place but ultimately opened the way for a new wave of academic expatriation across the Pacific from the mid-1990s.

When I expatriated myself in 2000 I took a different path, following the trajectory of Inter-Asian Cultural Studies north to Hong Kong just three years after the enclave's return to China. There, as in many parts of the world, a long-term struggle over the terms of becoming 'national' was and is inextricable from the challenges of globalization and international policy-sharing in educational institutions (Morris 2010). With 13 years in China rather than the USA shaping my perspectives now, I am awed by the expansion we have seen of Australian *national* institutions, organizations and initiatives in higher education, the media, the arts, broadcasting and in cultural industries broadly conceived – with a National Education Reform Agreement for secondary schooling (the 'Gonski' reform) and a National Broadband Network scheme still contested as I write. This change is a concrete product of policy work as well as of representation campaigns and related shifts in consciousness, and in the first edition of *Making It National* (Turner 1994) Graeme began to consider in a systematic way the changing conditions in which that work was becoming possible. The 'it' nationalized in his title included the larrikin entrepreneurial culture unleashed by the deregulation of the Australian financial system under the Hawke Labor Government of 1983–1991. Paying close critical attention to popular representations of economic values, after earlier work devoted to 'national fictions' in literature and film (Turner 1986), *Making It National* importantly extended the project initiated by Donald Horne in a book that for me is the founding text of Cultural Studies in Australia, *Money Made Us* (Horne 1976). Writing almost 20 years after Horne's biting account, Graeme was able to 'multiply' Australian hypotheses about national identity by combining a critique of the public uses of nationalism by business heroes pursuing private gain with a positive vision of the democratic and diversifying potential of the media and the public cultural institutions that Horne's policy-minded generation had earlier begun to build.

Another two decades down the track since *Making It National* first appeared, we have seen much un-making as well as remaking of the national during the globalizing years in between. Throughout this period Graeme has documented, analysed and above all generated new ideas for 'making it national' in concrete areas of cultural practice. Within higher education in particular, Graeme Turner has played a role that has extended his influence well beyond our discipline – in the process helping to give Cultural Studies an institutional heft and solidity in Australia that is rare in Western contexts although increasingly achieved in parts of Asia (Morris and Hjort 2012). As President of the Australian Academy of the Humanities (2005–2007), for example, he indefatigably and with much success lobbied a hostile federal government to recognize the social and economic claims of the Arts and Humanities to relevance for our national life. Subsequently, he served consecutive terms from 2008 on the Prime Minister's Science, Engineering and Innovation Council as only the second Humanities scholar to be appointed to that influential body. I can attest from experience in Hong Kong how frequently he has been called upon in the Inter-Asian world as an expert adviser for universities involved in their own struggle to 'make it national' in education while absorbing the imperatives of a globalizing policy sphere. At Lingnan University alone he acted for three years (2003–2006) as External Examiner for our BA Cultural Studies programme (2003–2006), helping us revise in practical detail our approach to assessment strategies, and then gave postgraduates as well as academic staff advice on coping with changes in higher education policy during intensive visits in 2009 and 2012.

In his institution-building work as well as his writing and teaching, Graeme puts into meticulous and exacting practice the ideal of 'constructing common ground' (Turner 1991, p. 27) so often invoked as a goal of activism in the academy as well as in our wider political life. It is easy to end an article rhetorically waving at that ideal, but GT pulls off the remarkable feat of doing it in reality –even in such inhospitable corners of our reality as the corridors of power in Canberra. How does he do this, when many of us find it hard to make common ground with colleagues in other factions of Cultural Studies, never mind in other academic disciplines or with scientists? No doubt being a certain kind of Aussie bloke has helped GT survive the scrums they have in those corners, but many a bloke can hang in there without scoring something real for our sector. I think Graeme's genius is very much a matter of 'creativity in the gaps'. Graeme is a play-maker. Whether coming down the middle or veering towards the wing, he is always on the look-out for that chance to come up with something special, making opportunities for action where none are supposed to exist. Those opportunities are not only occasions to have input to university or government policy, important as these occasions are along with the interventions in the public sphere that he once called 'passing on the benefits' of theoretical critique (Turner 1996, p. 14). Opportunities are also chances that a great player *produces* in the gap between policy and its implementation. This gap is temporal as well as situational; while its duration, form and potential will differ with conditions, it is in the nature of the institutional game that the gap will always arise and something unforeseen can occur. The second aspect of Graeme's genius is then his clarity of purpose. As I see it, his game has always been about renewing both the principle and the real possibility of practising education as a 'public good', a value he has recently defined as 'the idea that there is an intellectual, ethical-moral purpose behind the production and distribution of knowledge that is directed towards the social and cultural wellbeing of a society, and not just its economic development' (Turner 2012, p. 104).

Neoliberal times are not meant to be propitious for promoting social and cultural well-being at taxpayers' expense. A third aspect of Graeme's way of doing what he does may explain why he has been able to pursue his purpose so effectively. This is his active solidarity with others as a scholar, as a teacher and as a 'public servant' in the old honorific sense of the term. Creativity in the gaps is not a self-centring practice; the play-maker's art is often hidden from casual spectators as he (or she) drops back to send someone else over the line. Graeme has assumed many roles in order to support and enable other people through his institution-building; a solid full-back when he is needed, he is also a heavy forward and a dazzling try-scorer combined. In recent years he has excelled at high-level coaching, most obviously through his creation of the Centre for Critical and Cultural Studies, where under his leadership (1999–2012) early career researchers and mature scholars alike could enjoy the time and the conditions for shaping or renewing their professional vocations. I speak as a beneficiary of Graeme's coaching skills: when I first became a Head of Department he taught me how to fill my diary in advance so I could choose what meetings I might be 'free' to attend, thus preserving my good temper for the benefit of all. Years later, a month spent reading and writing at his Centre reminded me why I became an academic and decided me to stay in Australia. Multiplied through the lives of all the people he has helped, guided and backed up over the years, this kind of coaching has national quality impact; there should be a special performance indicator for government to recognize its worth. Graeme's is a *practical* and personal politics of promoting 'well-being' on a daily basis, and this is one of the reasons why even his most ambitious institutional experiments generally work. Academics now positioned as 'research stars' do not always understand this or the complexity of the work it takes. To shape a discipline it's not enough to build personal fame, raise grants or score big 'points' at research evaluation time. You need loving kindness and solidarity with staff at all levels. You need a wide range of versatile skills and the speed and finesse to use them well; and, come rain, hail or shine in the institution you work for, you have to turn up to play.

As other essays in this issue attest, Graeme's career has been one of continuous movement between pedagogy, research, criticism, policy, administration, management and diverse kinds of mentoring. In sports we could call him the 'total package' but in Australian university jargon this range of capacities is now rather feebly linked to a figure called the 'all-round academic' – a consolation descriptor, as though having a single edge ('research only') is better than the trifecta of excellence in teaching, research and service. How misguided can we be? Sometimes I think this increasingly internalized misguiding is a conspiracy to ensure that in the future we may have no visionary, practical leaders of the Humanities who are, like Graeme, top-notch teachers and scholars as well. I believe that 'research only' pursued for more than a few successive years tends to make us stupid in cultural domains. We hear a lot, and rightly so, about the importance of research to teaching but the importance of teaching to the formulation of original research is gravely underestimated. We are not scientists in this decisive way: without the discipline of encountering new cultural influences in that 'public' space of a classroom, we very quickly lose touch with the social worlds we imagine ourselves addressing as well as analysing when we write.

The depth of Graeme's pedagogical skill shows not only in his copious and brilliant provision of textbooks but above all in the longevity of his multiply revised and re-issued texts. As I write, after 23 years *British Cultural Studies* is in its third edition and selling out of Amazon with 'more on the way'. My personal favourite and long-term stand-by for teaching undergraduate courses in cinema is *Film as Social Practice* (Turner 1988), now in its fourth edition and selling out after a quarter of a century. Using it annually to teach in Hong Kong, I would sometimes look for a different textbook for a change. I never found a substitute, and this is why. *Film as Social Practice* really is written for students, not for the politically monitoring gaze of colleagues. It is a book for people who want to learn directly about film and society, not about where the author stands in a range of esoteric disciplinary debates or what he or she thinks about Heidegger, Foucault and Derrida. Remarkably few 'textbooks' in Cultural Studies can meet this classroom relevance test for a context where students are reading in English as a second or third language (that is, the context of most students in the world) in countries where the configuration of disciplines and hence debate about what matters differs greatly from the Western Anglophone tradition. While my students often failed to recognize the English titles of the films the book discusses, furtively referring to the photocopied Chinese translations hidden under their desks, the plain and beautiful prose of *Film as Social Practice* never failed to inspire them to think for themselves.

At the same time, Graeme has a much more complex attitude than I do to the establishment of a national infrastructure for research production and evaluation, having been involved directly in building much of what we have through his work for the Australian Research Council and the learned Academies as well as the University of Queensland. I would certainly be just one of many Australian academics to regard his brilliant invention and convening (2005–2010) of the Australian Research Council Cultural Research Network (CRN) as one of his greatest achievements. Federally funded, the CRN worked on two fronts: it put emerging as well as mid-career researchers in collaborative relationships across the continent at a time when travel funding had become sparse to procure; and it made scholars in Cultural Studies work productively with geographers, anthropologists, historians and social scientists. Despite my admiration, however (and my participation on the CRN's International Advisory Board), we did recently manage to have a bit of biff over what I stubbornly and not altogether rationally regard as the over-valuation in Australia of research relative to teaching. At a symposium hosted by Monash University's 'Prato Centre' in Italy,[5] I went into one of my favourite rants about why the sidelining of textual analysis in research funding-driven Cultural Studies reflects the devaluing of teaching as a vocation (Morris 2006). My argument is that the 'close reading' of texts was primarily a way of teaching people to *write*. Graeme, whose task was to explain the current research development framework to emerging scholars, noted sternly (having taught thousands more students than I ever will): 'that might be so, but that's the way it is'. No doubt because we had all enjoyed an outdoor screening the night before of Baz Luhrmann's *Australia*, in which these lines of dialogue occur, I flounced back: 'just because that's how it is that doesn't mean it should be'. Alas: on balance I have to admit that my Nicole Kidman is an epic fail while GT squares up pretty well as Hugh Jackman.

His own research, as it happens, has always been engaged with the *question* of 'what should be?' in Australian cultural and media scholarship. He has a demanding view of what kinds of research that scholarship involves. Long ago he frightened me off writing a book about Australian TV drama with an eloquent argument that to understand television you have to study the lot, not just pick out the bits you find aesthetically engaging; his example of the knowledge it takes to be credible as a TV scholar happened to be my pet horror at the time – gardening shows. Practising as well as preaching this rigorous approach to constructing an 'intellectual project' (Turner 1996, p. 7), Graeme has over the years been able to produce an internationally influential body of scholarship that excels at constituting real *objects* of study along with concepts that others can carry into different empirical fields: celebrity, tabloidism, the changing role of news and current affairs in nation-formation, the 'demotic turn' (Turner 2010) to reality and opinion genres, 'post-broadcast' television (Turner and Tay 2006) and, most recently, the challenge of writing situated ethnographies of its consumption (Pertierra and Turner 2013). Through all of Graeme's work two institutional complexes, the media and education, encounter, test and creatively modify each other; in the process, bringing to Humanities-trained scholars a new model of what research could mean.

As Phil Gould always says of a brilliant player: 'oh, he's a thinker, that boy! He's … a thinker'. In no area is Graeme's conceptual creativity more evident than in the so-called service domain. Graeme has shown us that service need not only be a matter of 'doing the hard yards', a necessary grind – although it certainly is that too. Service as Graeme has practised it is the very medium in which we can develop effective strategies in academic life for what Gould calls 'the modern game'. Theorists of modernity might well pay attention to Gould's usage of that phrase. Gould thinks of modernity as Lyotard does; the beginning of the *modern* game in League is recurrent, and can be traced to whatever changes in rules and tactics that Gould has in mind for a particular argument. At big picture level we can trace the modern university game in Australia to the Dawkins (1988) report, with its call to tie tertiary education in Australia more closely to the needs of industry and national productivity. In the ensuing 25 years, however, we have seen an unending series of transformations in the game, following changes in government, in the placing of the tertiary education portfolio, in university leadership and organization, or simply in the composition of committees. Throughout this Graeme kept his eye on the ball and taught us by example the importance of getting involved, rather than hanging round the sidelines whinging. This is the true meaning of that great sporting cliché, 'turning up to play'. It does not mean, cynically, 'you have to be in it to win it', although that is a logical precondition of any play at all. It means, participating in the effort with all of your heart and soul. Graeme's great gift as a leader is *exemplary*: he is able to show us what is possible on the basis of what he has learned and striven for himself, teaching us how to grasp changes in the rules, keep our eyes on the ball of what matters, and imagine new moves that are not supposed to be possible – how to find that gap opening up where creativity is possible, while not 'surrendering the space' (Turner 2011) that has already been made by Cultural Studies towards achieving the goal of the public good.

In the correspondence to organize this Symposium, Gay Hawkins explicitly asked the participants not to use PowerPoint for our presentations. It had never occurred to me to do that but as soon as I read Gay's request I began to imagine what my ideal PowerPoint for Graeme might be like. In no time at all I was envisaging a four-wall multimedia spectacle on the scale of Suncorp Stadium packed out for a Broncos game. On each wall, footage would be playing of great moments in the careers of four of my own favourite Queensland players, each of whom could exemplify an aspect of Graeme's achievement. On one wall would be the mighty Mal Meninga, making the stadium shake as he ran the length of the field to thunder over the line in a State of Origin match best forgotten by a New South Wales person like me. On the second wall, Gordon Tallis (my favourite Bronco) scrapping and dodging impossibly through a melee of players so terrified of his ferocity that most of them fell over. On the third wall, Petero Civoniceva, the endurance player who in 2009 had played the most international matches for Australia of any forward in history and who seemed always able to get up again no matter how many hard knocks he took. And on the fourth wall, Graeme's favourite: 'King' Wally Lewis, the wise one; the inspiring sportsman whose kindness and courtesy made him beloved even by those who played against him. For the soundtrack to my multimedia tribute to Graeme Turner, there is of course only one possibility: Tina Turner singing the song that she made an Australian Rugby League anthem before it was lifted by football codes and clubs worldwide – 'Simply the Best'.

Disclosure statement

No potential conflict of interest was reported by the author.

Notes

1   Broadly about the relationship of Australian Studies to Cultural Studies, this
     debate went on for several years. See Morris 1990a, 1991, Turner,
     1991, 1996.
2   In an early article for Cultural Studies I used the example of Rugby League to
     discuss the constraints imposed on the language of Australian Cultural Studies
     by the conventions of a British or American-based 'international refereed
     journal' (Morris 1992). Mercifully today we have Wikipedia (see 'Glossary of
     Rugby League terms').
3   On these two players, respectively, see Knox (2013) and McGregor (2004).
     Knox plausibly describes Sonny Bill Williams as a 'consultant superhero, the
     model fly-in, fly-out free-lancer for these globalised times' (p. 2). Where
     Williams switches between sports and football codes as well as between clubs,
     Lewis had a deep commitment to Rugby League in Queensland and to the
     Brisbane Broncos club. See also Headon (1999).
4   The first four issues of the journal are available online through Curtin
     University   at   http://humanities.curtin.edu.au/schools/MCCA/ccs/ajcs_
     journal.cfm
5   This symposium was Offshore Processes: International Perspectives on
     Australian Film and Television, organized by Therese Davis and Liz Conor,
     Monash Prato Centre, Italy, 8–11 July 2012.

References

Chesterton, R. (1996) *Good as Gould: Phil Gould's Stormy Life in Football*, Sydney,
     Ironbark.
Dawkins, J. S. (1988) *Industry Training in Australia: The Need for Change*, Canberra,
     Department of Employment, Education and Training, http://hdl.voced.edu.
     au/10707/142028 (accessed 3 December 2013).

Fiske, J., Hodge B. & Turner, G. (1988) *Myths of Oz: Reading Australian Popular Culture*, Sydney, Allen & Unwin.

Foss, P., ed. (2009) *The & -Files: Art & text 1981–2002*, Brisbane, QLD and Florida, FL, Institute of Modern Art and Whale and Star.

Frow, J. (2005) 'Australian cultural studies: theory, story, history', *Australian Humanities Review*, vol. 37, http://www.australianhumanitiesreview.org/archive/Issue-December-2005/frow.html (accessed 14 August 2013).

'Glossary of rugby league terms', *Wikipedia*, http://en.wikipedia.org/wiki/Glossary_of_rugby_league_terms (accessed 1 April 2013).

Gould, P. (2013) 'Here's to you, Mr Robinson', *The Sydney Morning Herald League HQ*, 14 April, http://www.smh.com.au/rugby-league/league-news/heres-to-you-mr-robinson-20130413-2hsbs.html (accessed 16 April 2013).

Grossberg, L., Nelson, C. & Treichler, P., eds (1992) *Cultural Studies*, New York, NY and London, Routledge.

Headon, D. (1999) 'Up from the ashes: the phoenix of a rugby league literature', *Football Studies*, vol. 2, no. 2, pp. 100–114, http://library.la84.org/Sports-Library/FootballStudies/1999/FS0202i.pdf (accessed 20 October 2013).

Hodsdon. B. (2001) *Straight Roads and Crossed Lines: The Quest for Film Culture in Australia from the 1960s?*, Shenton Park, WA, Bernt Porridge.

Horne, D. (1976) *Money Made Us*, Harmondsworth and Ringwood, Penguin Books.

Knox, M. (2013) 'League cannot drop its pants to keep SBW', *The Sydney Morning Herald*, Weekend Sport, 14–15 September, p. 2.

McGregor, A. (2004) *Wally Lewis: Forever the King*, St Lucia, University of Queensland Press.

Morris, M. (1990a) 'A small serve of spaghetti', *Meanjin*, vol. 49, no. 3, pp. 470–480.

Morris, M. (1990b) 'Banality in Cultural Studies', in *Logics of Television*, ed. P. Mellencamp, Bloomington, IN, Indiana University Press, pp. 14–43.

Morris, M. (1991) 'Response to Graeme Turner', *Meanjin*, vol. 50, no. 1, pp. 32–34.

Morris, M. (1992) 'Afterthoughts on Australianism', *Cultural Studies*, vol. 6, no. 3, pp. 468–475.

Morris, M. (2005) 'On the future of parochialism: globalization, *Young and Dangerous IV*, and cinema studies in Tuen Mun', in *Film History and National Cinema: Studies in Irish Film II*, eds. J. Hill & K. Rockett, Dublin, Four Courts Press, pp. 17–36.

Morris, M. (2006) 'From criticism to research: the textual in the academy', *Cultural Studies Review*, vol. 12, no. 2, pp. 17–32.

Morris, M. (2010) 'On English as a Chinese Language: implementing globalization', in *Universities in Translation: the Mental Labor of Globalization*, ed. B. de Bary, Hong Kong, Hong Kong University Press, pp. 177–196.

Morris, M. & Hjort, M., eds. (2012) *Creativity and Academic Activism: Instituting Cultural Studies*, Hong Kong, Durham, NC, and London, Hong Kong University Press and Duke University Press.

Murray, S., ed. (1980) *The New Australian Cinema*, Melbourne, Nelson/Cinema Papers.

Pertierra, A. C. & Turner, G. (2013) *Locating Television: Zones of Consumption*, Milton Park and New York, NY, Routledge.

'Phil Gould' http://www.icmi.com.au/phil-gould (accessed 12 August 2013).

Sangster, G., ed. (1987) *Sighting References: Ciphers, Systems and Codes in Recent Australian Visual Art*, Sydney, Artspace. Available at: ICMI Speakers and Entertainers.

Turner, G. (1986) *National Fictions: Literature, Film, and the Construction of Australian Narrative*, Sydney, Allen & Unwin.

Turner, G. (1988) *Film as Social Practice*, 2nd edn, 1993. 3rd edn, 1999. 4th edn, 2006. London, Routledge.

Turner, G. (1990) *British Cultural Studies: An Introduction*, Boston, MA, Unwin Hyman.

Turner, G. (1991) 'Return to Oz: populism, the academy and the future of Australian studies, *Meanjin*, vol. 50, no. 1, pp. 19–31.

Turner, G. (1994) *Making It National: Nationalism and Australian Popular Culture*, Sydney, Allen & Unwin.

Turner, G. (1996) 'Discipline wars: Australian studies, cultural studies and the analysis of national culture', *Journal of Australian Studies*, vol. 20, no. 50–51, pp. 6–17.

Turner, G. (2004) *Understanding Celebrity*, London, Thousand Oaks, CA and New Delhi, SAGE.

Turner, G. (2010) *Ordinary People and the Media: the Demotic Turn*, London, Thousand Oaks, CA and New Delhi, Sage Publications.

Turner, G. (2011) 'Surrendering the space: convergence culture, cultural studies and the curriculum', *Cultural Studies*, vol. 25, no. 4–5, pp. 685–699.

Turner, G. (2012) *What's Become of Cultural Studies?* London, Thousand Oaks, CA and New Delhi, SAGE.

Turner, G. and Tay, J., eds. (2006) *Television Studies after TV: Understanding Television in the Post-broadcast Era*, Milton Park and New York, NY, Routledge.

Toby Miller

DEPENDENCIA MEETS GENTLE NATIONALISM

The dominant historiography of Australian cultural studies assumes that the south-east of the country, where its major population centres are located, is crucial to the field's formation. That account also problematizes nationalism. This article offers a counter-narrative, based in dependencia theory. It argues for the centrality to cultural studies of two peripheral cities in Australia where Graeme Turner made his mark, and of his particular contribution, 'gentle nationalism'.

Introduction

This volume is a critical celebration of Graeme Turner's contribution to cultural studies. As such, it belongs to a particular genre, namely the *Festschrift* or *liber amicorum*. The rules of such writing are fairly straightforward, though they are not generally codified: honour the faculty member in question and take up some of his or her ideas. In that spirit, I'm not going to cite works produced by other folks that form the dominant alternative to my version. So the historiography of Australian cultural studies to which I refer is, perhaps maddeningly, left up to readers to find, should they so wish. Maybe I'm creating this object from a straw man, as one says in the USA, or an Aunt Sally, in a differently gendered British tradition.[1]

This article offers a counter-narrative (if anyone still uses such terms) to the usual ones. It argues for the centrality to cultural studies in the 1980s of two quasi-peripheral Australian cities where Graeme made his mark (Perth and Brisbane) and similarly peripheral institutions nested within those cities (new universities, institutes of technology and colleges of advanced education) along with the work of people who travelled far and wide to transcend parochial norms.[2]

My second argument is that key faculty members who established this initial formation developed and played with cultural nationalism. Such commitments are easy to mock and criticize, but may function quite differently from how they are portrayed. Like many of his era, Graeme's is a (comparatively) gentle nationalism, in contrast to the anti-nationalism that is assumed to be crucial for Australian cultural studies.

I take him to be both indexical and constitutive of each tendency – a figure from the margins and a critical agent of gentle nationalism. To make my case, I draw on *dependencia* theory and offer an account of his path-breaking work on Australian literature and cinema, *National Fictions* (1993a).

Core and periphery

The basis for my analysis is perhaps the most powerful and enduring theoretical export to have emerged from the Global South: *dependencia*. *Dependistas* took their cue from Raúl Prebisch (1950, 1982), whose theory, research and leadership inspired the Economic Commission for Latin America and the United Nations Conference on Trade and Development (UNCTAD). UNCTAD became the most important international institution problematizing imperial domination. It provided decolonizing nations and recently freed ones with a forum to query the Global North's dominant narrative of development through national institutions and the free movement of capital.

The conventional version of development peddled solipsistic accounts of world politics, economics and culture that extrapolated from mythic explanations for the growth of the Global North. Its economic guide was VietNam War bombing advocate Walt Rostow (1960) and its representatives in political science included his fellow Cold Warriors Lucien Pye and Sidney Verba (1965).

By contrast, UNCTAD, Prebisch, and their kind worked with notions of dependent underdevelopment and structural inequality to explain why many parts of the world had not achieved the economic take-off that was predicted and prescribed by orthodox social scientists. *Dependistas* focused on the expropriation of natural resources and human labour by wealthy nations from poor ones thanks to their historical, military, governmental and commercial dominance and called for a New International Economic Order and a New World Information and Communication Order (Higgott and Robison 1985, Higgott 1993). Their critique of capitalist modernization maintained that the transfer of technology, politics and economics had become unattainable, because multinational corporations united business and govern-mental interests and power to regulate cheap labour markets, produce new consumers and guarantee pliant employees (Reeves 1993, pp. 24–25, 30).

For radical intellectuals formed in the 1970s, these were key terms of debate, along with feminism, ideology, hegemony and class struggle. But despite *dependencia*'s analytical force, it never attained hegemony in policy debates, and *dependistas* have taken different turns since. Some moved towards the New International Division of Labor to account for the economic growth enjoyed by East Asian states that mobilized their reserve armies of labour to manufacture goods for the Global North (Fröbel *et al.* 1980). Others were attracted by neoliberalism, because of a desire to elude, by any means possible, the horrors of dictatorship and the financial punishment meted out to leftist governments by international markets (Cardoso 2005). A third group favoured a fuller-throated Marxist anti-imperialism (Amin 1997). The theory was also criticized for focusing on state and economy to the exclusion of culture (Mignolo 2012; but see Wallerstein 1989).

Despite this splintering, *dependencia* continues to invigorate debate among progressives. And its awareness of spatially and historically induced inequality offers a means of understanding semi-peripheral, semi-metropolitan nations such as Australia – wealthy but weak, worried and weary, arrogant yet anxious, vexed while vested. The country has dependent cultural relations with the USA and UK and economic ones with those nations plus China and Japan. Born from post-imperial protectionism and dependent for its development on being a farm and a quarry, Australia embodies the Dutch Disease (Ebrahim-Zadeh 2003) so fully that it generated the Gregory (1976) Thesis, which explains that capital investment and state reliance on natural resources preclude the development of industries that add value through the talent of labour.

A variety of cultural analysis has used dependency theory to understand both Australian society and its importation of popular culture (Gray and Lawrence 2001, Cunningham 2008). The centre–periphery axis of power is expressed in terms of capital formation, population, politics and cultural production. Australia's south-east corner hosts its supreme court, seat of political power, media networks and banks, for instance. And it's significant that the Australian Broadcasting Corporation has long referred, both dismissively and organizationally, to the 'BAPH states', i.e. BrisbaneAdelaidePerthHobart.

Graeme's scholarly trajectory embodies Australia's place in the world system. His studies took him from Sydney to Canada (Queen's University in Kingston) then the UK (the University of East Anglia in Norwich); a familiar *Bildungsroman*[3] in which heroes and heroines move from the suburbs to downtown to campus, then from a marginal academic country to more powerful ones. Other examples among the founders of Australian cultural studies include Stuart Cunningham going from Brisbane to Montréal before Madison; Noel King leaving Newcastle for Kingston then Adelaide for Cardiff; Bob Hodge ex Perth to Cambridge and Norwich; Stephen Muecke and Anne Freadman heading to Paris after Melbourne and Meaghan Morris and Paul Patton doing so from Sydney; John Frow departing Canberra for Buenos Aires, Ithaca and Heidelberg; Jennifer Craik moving from Canberra to Cambridge; and so on.

What did these travellers encounter and bring back on their return? Foundational figures and debates from Habermas to Halliday, discourse to deconstruction, Foucault to Frankfurt, Lacan to Lyotard, Bourdieu to Baudrillard, Derrida to Deleuze and Birmingham to the BFI. A recombinatory verve saw them look to blend rather than choose between tendencies, formations and schools, thereby evading such banal oppositions as *Screen* versus the Centre for Contemporary Cultural Studies or comp. lit *contra* comm. studies.

Such movements are colonial: they assume in some way that real knowledge – or benefit – exist elsewhere, but that while such folks may leave in order to learn, they will probably also return, whether or not that was their original intention. Because within, they remain what they were born into, however hard to define and appreciate that may be (in Graeme's case and those above, an Australian). It reminds me of Latin Americans undertaking graduate education abroad then going home: Néstor García Canclini (Buenos Aires–Paris), Anamaria Tamayo Duque (Medellín–Riverside), Daniel Mato (Buenos Aires–Brighton), André Dorcé Ramos (Mexico City–London), Jesús Arroyave Cabrera (Barranquilla–Piscataway–Miami), Paula López Caballero (Mexico City–Paris), Bianca Freire Medeiros (Rio de Janeiro–Binghamton), Ismail Xavier (São Paolo–New York City), Akuavi Adonon Viveros (Mexico City–Paris), Olivia Gall (Mexico City–Grenoble), Paulina Aroch Fugellie (Mexico City–Amsterdam), Bruno Campanella (Rio de Janeiro–London), Luz María Sánchez (Guadalajara–Barcelona), Ana María Ochoa Gautier (Bogotá–Bloomington), Aimée Vega Montiel (Mexico City–Barcelona), Erna von der Walde (Bogotá–Frankfurt–Colchester), Rodrigo Gómez García (Mexico City–Barcelona), Guillermo Mastrini (Buenos Aires–Madrid), Guillermo Orozco Gómez (Guadalajara–Cambridge, MA), Benjamín Mayer Foulkes (Mexico City–Brighton) and Claudia Arroyo Quiroz (Mexico City–London).

This pluralism also operated in reverse, among people who moved to Australia, learning about local conditions while holding onto their backgrounds. Consider such names as Horst Ruthrof, Vijay Mishra, Jon Stratton, Tony Bennett, David Rowe, David Saunders, Sophie Watson, Ghassan Hage, Theo van Leeuwen, Gunther Kress, Lesley Stern, Jim McKay, Pal Ahluwalia, Eric Michaels, Bill Routt, Ron Burnett, Hart Cohen, Alan Mansfield, Gordon Tait, Simon During, Colin Mercer, Noel Sanders, Krishna Sen, Michael O'Toole, Albert Moran, David Wills, Elspeth Probyn, Ien Ang, Alec McHoul, Rita Felski, Susan Melrose, and the Johns Tulloch, Fiske, and Hartley.[4] Each of these folks seemed to appreciate or identify with Australianness in all its polysemic prolixity, and to do so with alacrity and wit as well as critique. And most taught at second- and third-tier schools.

An awareness of core–periphery inequality as per UNCTAD et al. runs through the rich exchanges of this formation. Folks who departed temporarily to test or improve themselves, or who arrived from elsewhere, may not have seen Australia as suffering in the way that classic subjects and objects of empire did, but they recognized and experienced national and international core–periphery relations of inequality, due to their addresses, accents, genders, phenotypes, delights and emotions. That enriched their analyses of class, race and gender in a demographically small nation that was encased in a settled, settler whiteness, but located in a very different part of the world geographically, linguistically, religiously and ethnically. In reaction to this, some (though not all of them) saw a contingent utility in nationalism, of which more below.

As noted above, these intellectuals mostly worked outside the metropoles of Australian higher education, renowned Research One schools such as Sydney, Melbourne and the Australian National University. Graeme was eventually claimed by the University of Queensland, one of the so-called Sandstone Six (the nation's first universities, one in each state capital). But like almost everyone I mentioned above, Graeme spent a lot of time in an historically subordinate sector that was more open to media, communication and cultural studies than these storied locales.

Until a supposedly meritocratic reform in the late 1980s that in fact did nothing to alter the class divisions of higher education, there were three types of degree-granting institution in Australia, each of them public. (Although education was, and remains, constitutionally the creature of the states, in keeping with the US example, policies governing universities and the funds financing them have mostly come from the Federal Government.)

The three Australian forms were universities, institutes of technology and colleges of advanced education. The first of these groups was meant to create new knowledge and provide undergraduate instruction across the arts, sciences and social sciences as well as doctoral education. The second emerged to undertake highly applied tasks, notably the production of engineers. The third was principally responsible for teacher training. Unsurprisingly, the humanities and soft social sciences in these vocational institutions were subordinate components of sectors that were themselves subordinate – offering the Australian equivalent of breadth requirements. The reforms that merged the three groups a quarter of a century ago have not really erased these distinctions other than in name, although everyone now hands out PhDs and is 'excellent'.

During the 1980s, humanities fields within institutes of technology and colleges of advanced education – to repeat, rather peripheral elements of rather peripheral institutions – were crucial to the emergence of cultural studies, as were two universities (Griffith in Brisbane and Murdoch in Perth[5]) that were 1970s upstarts situated outside the south-eastern corridor of Australian political-economic power. These various schools were dedicated, in keeping with their genesis, to what used to be called 'problem-solving'. It was crucial to their promotion of interdisciplinarity rather than the parthenogenesis of traditional academic subjects.

As such, they recruited people from the cutting edge of cultural studies. For example, Fiske left Britain for the Western Australian Institute of Technology (now Curtin University), where Graeme also worked. Kress, King and Muecke taught at one of South Australia's federated colleges of advanced education. Frow, Melrose, Mishra, O'Toole, Moran, Bill Green, Mitzi Goldman, Johnny Darling, Rod Giblett, Niall Lucy, Stern, Ruthrof, Felski, Hodge, Hartley, Ang, McHoul and Tom O'Regan were at Murdoch. Ian Hunter, Bennett, Cunningham, McHoul, Stratton, Saunders, King, Sylvia Lawson, Pat Laughren, Jonathan Dawson, Dugald Williamson, Moran, Mick Counihan, Stern and O'Regan were at Griffith. Like Graeme, Cunningham moved to Brisbane's Queensland Institute of Technology (now Queensland University of Technology).

As part of these peripheral trajectories, the founders of Australian cultural studies were heavily involved in teaching undergraduates rather than graduates, and generally published without articulation to research grants. They were closer to the productive marginality of cultural studies in the US communication studies of big mid-western state schools than the headline-grabbing but derivative textual analysis proliferating in the Ivies.

In keeping with that lineage, we might consider here the creatively synthetic side of Graeme's publishing output, which exemplifies his experience teaching large undergrad classes. The popular and effective textbooks *British Cultural Studies* (Turner 2002) and *Film as Social Practice* (Turner 2006) have been revised and reprinted, and his edited collection on cultural studies (Turner 1993b) is also influential.

Scholars like Graeme frequently blended appearances in leading overseas journals and monograph series with participation in and administration of alternative, activist publishing projects that were neither for profit nor recognition, such as the late lamented *Australian Journal of Cultural Studies* (http://wwwmcc. murdoch.edu.au/ReadingRoom/serial/AJCS/AJCSindex.html). Scholarly specialization, self-promotion and parthenogenesis were not goals, as far as I could tell. These folks made their careers and names by accident, collaboration and productivity rather than design, desire, calculation or competition. Put another way, the scientific metrication of pedagogic and publishing quality and quantity and accompanying *assujettissement* as 'early career', 'junior' or 'research' academics that govern so much of contemporary higher education did not determine their activities. Rather, a can-do spirit of invention, brilliance and commitment did so. Teaching and research were inextricably linked, and hierarchies among faculty were resolutely disobeyed.

The conditions of existence for such tendencies formed a peculiar conjuncture: Murdoch, Griffith and some of the institutes and colleges were planned and built in the late 1960s and early 1970s – years of plenty. But their doors opened around the same time as oil shocks and stagflation broke down the post-War Keynesian consensus, ushering in austerity. The fiscal crisis meant that jobs at established universities were hard to find for emergent Australian intellectuals. Then the anti-university policies of the Thatcher government drove UK-based scholars abroad. The combination of these two forces was paradoxically bountiful for the periphery. They let young people in young institutions (somewhat) loose beyond the romper room. Courses were taught, often collaboratively, by folks whose knowledge arched across ethnomethodology, literary theory, art, political economy, performance, women's studies, public policy, communications, history and philosophy. Filmmakers operated alongside critics, ethnographers next to semioticians, *littérateurs* with political economists. People enjoyed the contestation of differing perspectives. Buying out of teaching – or not teaching at all – was inconceivable and teaching without requiring students to do large amounts of reading was implausible. Work that abjured simultaneous theorization and empirical grounding was unthinkable.

And these folks were driven by an implicit leftism. They were mostly pro-democratic, pro-popular-culture feminist socialists, and they liked, as much as they doubted, the institutions of learning and pleasure that employed them and they were deconstructing. Core–periphery inequalities were constitutive components of these formations, interpersonally, intellectually and institution-ally. How odd what I have just written may seem today, when the new right of cultural studies parlays the creative industries, film people favour apolitical formalism, cybertarians celebrate every Australian firm in the newer media while abjuring elderly and middle-aged ones, and leading scholars cannot find the large lecture halls on campus.

Gentle nationalism

The other crucial element that connected many, if not all, these thinkers, was their interest in the Australianness – whatever that might mean – of literature, film and television. They took their distance from US and the UK jingoism and were closer to critical Mexican cultural nationalism's wry, ironic, yet respectful stance towards foundational mythology and its cynical use by élites (García Canclini 1982).

Nationalism is routinely and rightly damned for its maleness, brutality, warmongering and other failings. But it has another history, as well, of longing for self-determination and resisting imperialism. The nation has been a core of post-colonialism, providing a means of registering claims for inclusion in both narratives and institutions.

I became aware of cultural studies and indeed Graeme's work in 1986, when his first book, *National Fictions*, appeared. In this last segment of the article, I'll focus on that volume's second edition (1993a). It sold many copies over an extended period in a successful career shift from topic-book to textbook, via the remarkable blend of original thought and exegetical expertise that is associated with Graeme.

It's strikingly apt that *National Fictions* underwent a visual transformation, from a K-Tel *Happening* '72 cover bursting with flags and a photo-montage of canonical masculinities, in edition one (figure 1) to edition two's Magritte/ Escher-like painting by Julia Ciccarone (figure 2) of a prost(r)ate man lying on his carefully chiselled floor, pulling a mountainous drape over himself from across a window pane that seems to be part of the bush. This is a movement from mo to pomo in the substitution of a supine, counter-realist figure for jingoistic kitsch, binding urban style to rural ideology.

Graeme's cultural nationalism is always conditional, careful and open-ended. His revisions underscore the contingent nature of semi-peripheral nationalism – why it can be democratizing and enabling as well as exclusionary and repressive. Graeme wants to know the morphology and life-course of the nation as they are realized in fictional narrative, a project that measures the country's desirable qualities against its less appealing ones. So his 1993 preface drew attention to the masculinist limits *and* utility of the bush *ethos* and how the increasing velocity of global cultural exchange brings into question stories of national identity.

National Fictions acknowledged the nation as a productive, not necessarily a good or bad object. This is somewhat counter to popular fabulations of cultural studies, which are woven around an anti-chauvinism that conventionally distinguishes itself from such affiliations. Graeme recognized that the concept of the nation, whilst always up for grabs, can be usefully redeployed in cultural policy, queer theory, racial diasporas, alternative television, small cinema and globalization.

National Fictions was before its time and set a standard. It spoke of an 'Australian accent'. This was not an expressive totality that encompassed the entire demographic reality of Australian life, a sign of organic harmony. Such claims are always forced and mystificatory. Rather, it was a metaphorical encapsulation, and the passage of time between 1986 and 1993 loosened Graeme from his formalist self and keen to identify the tropes that encouraged Australians to 'accept our social powerlessness' and 'inequities and divisions' as 'cause for concern' (1993a, pp. xiii–xiv; also see Turner 1994). This is a gentle nationalism.

The working assumptions underpinning *National Fictions* shift between a universal structural basis to narrative and the specificity of Australia as an axis of articulation and inflection, a site of 'values and beliefs' that take eponymised form in the book's title. This series of movements between the generic and the particular, the global and the local and the laws of narrative and their give-and-take (law and lore, *langue* and *parole*) provides a structural homology for the 'individual and society' debates that were conducted over utopian notions of Aboriginality in nineteenth-century European social theory, where human ideals were located in a lost past rather than an imagined future. For just as the Edenic primordialism of 'the first Australians' has long exercised cathectic extrapolations theory (Miller 2002), so the lost innocence of 'man' has been nostalgically positioned by local criticism in Australia's countryside, an organicist metaphor of equality, honesty and the coterminous ownership, control and practice of production.

National Fictions argues that film and literary criticism and history have extended these tropes into Australian binaries that encompass rurality and urbanism/nature and society and are outcomes of invading settler peoples making their way in a harsh landscape. But these binaries are again quite European. The book rightly invokes Romanticism as a way of conceptualizing an artistic and social disharmony of exile and discovery, of penury and pleasure.

This metaphor contrasts with the class-laden dross of urban existence. The exotic is brought to bear on the definition and survival of the familiar, such that

Australianness is found in the desert as well as the south-eastern seaboard. The natural environment's 'callous indifference' is a *leitmotif* (Turner 1993a, pp. 25, 28–29, 49).

National Fictions carefully traces the lineage of Australia's pastoral: authentic::urban:inauthentic divide while avoiding simplistic entrapment within it. Graeme is dubious about a critical and authorial preference for the rural as a proper site for metaphysical speculation. He sees equally useful stories emerging from the urban or post-apocalyptic world, often connected to the carceral history of the state. That is the site for civilizing influences and policies in the eyes of most critics, enacted on a slate of subjects, forced migrants, who are horrified by their testing-ground and conditions. The legacy of this history is a dialectic that mythically endorses 'the inevitability of subjection' even as it signifies freedom from the baleful Euro past and present that birthed and developed this escape/incarceration (1993a, pp. 31, 51, 54–55, 74–75). Graeme's appreciation of carceral life as central to society and ways of understanding it provides a valuable application of theorists as distinct as Michel Foucault and Angela Davis.

So, in some sense, he sets the pattern for Australian cultural studies seeing whiteness, confronting the alterity of the land and reminders of its 'clearance'. The nationalism he and others described may have been brutal, but their critical engagement with it supported a gentler, more self-aware form, just as their location in less populous and powerful parts of the country is an implicit metonym for Australian higher education and their own field.

Conclusion

Graeme Turner is a major figure of cultural studies, probably Australia's most-read exponent. His achievements and influence arch across numerous fields, and his syncretic innovations have enchanted – or at least focused – generations of undergrads. The fact that he does new thinking and synthesizing is a product both of years standing in front of hundreds of engineers and their vocational kind forced into humanities courses, and of the urge to meaningfulness and originality. In turn, those achievements derive from the contingencies and exigencies of core–periphery relations within Australian higher education. And the thoughtful, gentle nationalism that underpins Graeme's engagement with violent traditions of racial and gender domination permits a critical renovation of theories and commitments that will not disappear, despite myths of anti-nationalism, globalization and technological determinism.

And cultural studies in peripheral Australian institutions? It no longer relies on or thrives in them. Cultural studies has been successfully incorporated via the standing and hard work of Graeme and others into the Cultural Studies Association of Australia (http://www.csaa.asn.au/) and major institutions such as the Australian Research Council (http://www.arc.gov.au/media/releases/

media_27aug09.htm) and the Australian Academy of the Humanities (http://www.humanities.org.au/Fellowship/DisciplinarySections.aspx).

The older universities caught on and caught up. The stars I have listed generally left marginal places, where promotion was tough and they and their loved ones sometimes felt isolated. New funding schemes and managerial fashions militated against the cluster hiring necessary to regenerate what had been lost. As with many formations, it was transitory, fleeting even – but its mark can be seen in Graeme's work as a scholar, teacher and advocate.

Acknowledgement

Thanks to the editors for helpful criticisms and to an anonymous reviewer, who let me know that the essay's 'scholarship is pretty minimal' and its prose 'breezy'.

Disclosure statement

No potential conflict of interest was reported by the author.

Notes

1   My distinctive knowledge of Australian cultural studies is active up to 1993, when I was last a resident.
2   Subsequent cohorts have tended to study domestically, perhaps missing in the process the engagement with other languages and norms that were so crucial to this earlier group, while the belated but significant institutionalization of cultural studies in the nation's more venerable universities has seen some earlier pioneering places lag behind the status their avant-garde innovations merit.
3   Perhaps it would be appropriate to term this an Erziehungsroman.
4   As with other lists I have made here, I apologize for the exclusion of any other significant actors.
5   I worked at both of them during this period and am now employed by Murdoch for seven weeks a year.

References

Amin, S. (1997) *Capitalism in the Age of Globalization*, London, Zed Books.

Cardoso, F. H. (2005) 'Scholarship and statesmanship', *Journal of Democracy*, vol. 16, no. 2, pp. 5–12.

Cunningham, S. (2008) *In the Vernacular: A Generation of Australian Culture and Controversy*, St. Lucia, University of Queensland Press.

Ebrahim-Zadeh, C. (2003) 'Back to basics. Dutch disease: too much wealth managed unwisely', *Finance & Development*, vol. 40, no. 1. http://www.imf.org/external/pubs/ft/fandd/2003/03/ebra.htm.

Fröbel, F., Jürgen H. & Kreye, O. (1980) *The New International Division of Labor: Structural Unemployment in Industrialised Countries and Industrialisation in Developing Countries*, trans. P. Burgess, Cambridge, Cambridge University Press; Paris, Éditions de la Maison des Sciences de l'Homme.

García Canclini, N. (1982) *Las culturas populares en el capitalismo* [Popular Cultures under Capitalism], Mexico City, Nueva Imagen.

Gray, I. & Lawrence, G. (2001) *A Future for Regional Australia: Escaping Global Misfortune*, Melbourne, Cambridge University Press.

Gregory, R. G. (1976) 'Some implications of the growth of the mineral sector', *Australian Journal of Agricultural Economics*, vol. 20, pp. 71–91.

Higgott, R. (1993) *Political Development Theory: The Contemporary Debate*, London, Routledge.

Higgott, R. & Robison, R., eds. (1985) *Southeast Asia: Essays in the Political Economy of Structural Change*, London, Routledge & Kegan Paul.

Mignolo, W. (2012) *Local Histories/Global Designs: Coloniality, Subaltern Knowledges, and Border Thinking*, 2nd edn, Princeton, NJ, Princeton University Press.

Miller, T. (2002) 'A certain disservice', *Anthropological Quarterly*, vol. 75, no. 3, pp. 609–622.

Prebisch, R. (1950) *The Economic Development of Latin America and Its Principal Problems*, New York, United Nations.

Prebisch, R. (1982) *The Crisis of Capitalism and the Periphery: 1st Raúl Prebisch Lecture*, United Nations Conference on Trade and Development. http://www.rrojasdatabank.info/prebisch1st_prebisch_en.pdf.

Pye, L. W. & Verba, S., eds. (1965) *Political Culture and Political Development*, Princeton, NJ, Princeton University Press.

Reeves, G. (1993) *Communications and the 'Third World'*, London, Routledge.

Rostow, W. W. (1960) *The Stages of Economic Growth: A Non-communist Manifesto*, New York, Cambridge University Press.

Turner, G. (1993a) *National Fictions: Literature, Film and the Construction of Australian Narrative*, 2nd edn, Sydney, Allen & Unwin.

Turner, G., ed. (1993b) *Nation, Culture, Text: Australian Cultural and Media Studies*, London, Routledge.

Turner, G. (1994) *Making It National: Nationalism and Australian Popular Culture*, Sydney, Allen & Unwin.

Turner, G. (2002) *British Cultural Studies: An Introduction*, 3rd edn, Boston, MA, Unwin Hyman.

Turner, G. (2006) *Film as Social Practice*, 4th edn, London, Routledge.

Wallerstein, I. (1989) 'Culture as the ideological battleground of the modern world-system', *Hitotsubashi Journal of Social Studies*, vol. 21, no. 1, pp. 5–22.

Frances Bonner

KYLIE WILL BE OK

On the (im-)possibility of Australian celebrity studies

This article examines scholarly works published before and after Fame Games (2000) to investigate whether the development of Australian celebrity studies was one of the things that happened to Australian cultural studies. That book, written by Graeme Turner, P. David Marshall and Frances Bonner, observed the significance of an Australian celebrity's international profile to their national media coverage. Now, in an intellectual variant, Australian celebrity scholars disproportionately use foreign stars or Australians with international profiles to illustrate their arguments, with the exigencies of academic publishing providing one explanation. The article draws inter alia on Turner's several publications in the field in an attempt to discern whether there is an Australian inflection to celebrity studies or whether Australian scholars have been so significant in the international development of this subset of cultural studies that there is neither call nor space for a distinctively Australian approach.

It is with no little sense of hubris that I want to date the start of celebrity studies in Australia from the 2000 publication of *Fame Games: The Production of Celebrity in Australia*, of which I was a co-author with Graeme Turner and P. David Marshall (Turner *et al.* 2000). Internationally, the field could not easily be said to precede that time by much either. Many relevant books and articles were published prior to that, of course, but as contributions to other fields. Marshall's (2006) collection *The Celebrity Culture Reader* has as its earliest piece Max Weber's essay first published in 1922 on charismatic authority, followed by Daniel Boorstin's study of 'The Human Pseudo-event' first published in 1961. Its earliest Australian writing is John Langer's (1981) article on 'Television's "Personality System"'. None of these authors envisaged themselves as being located in celebrity studies, but in sociology, history or media studies. Altogether 26 of 41 chapters in that collection were published prior to 2000, and two of those were by Australian authors (not counting Marshall's written while he was not an Australian resident). It is clear just from this collection that much work had been done, in Australia as well as elsewhere, to provide a grounding on which the new field could draw.

This essay addresses the issue's theme by investigating the possibility that one thing that has happened to Australian cultural studies is the development of a sub-discipline, Australian celebrity studies. It considers Australian writing on celebrity, to which Turner has made such a substantial contribution, before and after that watershed date. It looks for any signs of change once the field became identifiable, having shifted from being just an area that media and cultural studies scholars, and some others, wrote on from their own disciplinary traditions. That celebrity studies is now an established arena for scholarly endeavour is clear; whether there is a recognizably Australian variant, less so. The major approach to identifying an Australian inflection to celebrity studies will involve considering the nationalities, arenas of renown and reception of the celebrities used by Australian scholars to illustrate their arguments. It seems a reasonable element given the importance to cultural studies work of context, here seen as the nation, its institutions and people. Certainly Australian audiences follow non-Australian celebrities; famous Australians are not a sine qua non for Australian celebrity studies, but they represent a straightforward place to start, not least because their production was at the heart of the *Fame Games* study.

The essay explores the establishment and location of celebrity studies in general, and some of Turner's own pronouncements on the field before considering the Australian scholarly setting into which *Fame Games* appeared. The survey of celebrity writings by Australian scholars before and after 2000 both looks at how the emergence of the field has had an impact on what is produced and explores the useful role in this of Australian celebrities of international standing, looking especially at the singer Kylie Minogue and animal adventurer Steve Irwin. Changes in international academic publishing have complicated the process of identifying the characteristics of a national sub-disciplinary shift. The essay concludes with the problem posed for a national inflection when many of its scholars are international leaders in the field.

The development and location of celebrity studies in and out of Australia

My nominating *Fame Games* as the first instance of Australian celebrity studies is retrospective. In the Introduction to the first chapter, we place our work as a contribution to media studies. The 1990s had been quite productive in terms of Australian books considering celebrities as part of their concerns. Two of them came from people who provided back cover endorsements for *Fame Games*. Catherine Lumby (1999), whose *Gotcha: Life in a Tabloid World* was identified as her qualification for comment there, and Mackenzie Wark (1999), whose *Celebrities, Culture and Cyberspace* functioned likewise, could jointly be seen as providing an alternative start date. I will discuss these and earlier books by John Langer (1998), the Re:Public (1997) collective and John Hartley (1996) later. The books were all located in media and/or cultural studies, but the appearance of so many in just four years is meaningful in terms of the field's coming into being. There had though been earlier precursors in a sequence of journal articles from the 1980s. They too will be examined later together with a perhaps more idiosyncratic precursor, Meaghan Morris's (1992) study of then Australian Treasurer, Paul Keating.

Marshall's (1997) *Celebrity and Power* is not in the list above since it was primarily written while he was still in Canada, from a disciplinary location in politics, and refers to Australia only in the Acknowledgements and the author's biography. The inclusion within Australian celebrity studies of works by a number of key authors – Marshall, Morris and Hartley, among those mentioned already – who published works dealing wholly or partly with celebrity while working in other countries attests both to academic mobility and just some of the difficulties at the heart of specifying a national inflection to a sub-disciplinary field. I follow Turner (1992) in seeing Australian cultural studies as 'cultural studies *in* Australia' (p. 426, his emphasis) and apply the formulation to Australian celebrity studies as well. First though I will consider the location of celebrity studies more generally.

A very common tracing of the genealogy of celebrity studies internationally begins in film studies with Richard Dyer's (1979) *Stars*. Almost immediately it was taken up beyond film. In Australia, Langer (1981) called on it, and Gabrielle O'Ryan and Brian Shoesmith (1987) show its continuing use by some Australian cultural studies scholars. Dyer had a strong influence on *Fame Games* too. In other countries key precursor works came from history (Boorstin 1987/ 1962), sociology (Alberoni 1962, Gamson 1994) or English (Braudy 1986, though English here encompasses cultural history and film). This disciplinary diversity was rarely the case in Australia.

I am thus probably on more contentious grounds in asserting that celebrity studies are a subset of cultural studies internationally than in Australia, though Marshall's naming his British and American Routledge reader a *Celebrity Culture* one supports this placement. Somewhat more equivocally, so does Turner's (2004) Preface to *Understanding Celebrity*, where he notes the limitations of cultural studies' consideration of celebrity as a field of representation before asserting his intention to consider also its production and consumption, but he still concludes by seeing celebrity as located firmly in culture. He maintains this belief in his contribution to the launch issue of *Celebrity Studies* (Turner 2010).

The public recognition of the existence of a scholarly field is usually marked some years after it has come into being by the publication of readers following publishers' recognizing that teaching in the area requires servicing. In addition to Marshall's mentioned above, Sean Redmond and Su Holmes' collection *Stardom and Celebrity: A Reader* appeared in 2007. The appearance of a dedicated journal is probably a final seal. The journal editors' foundational introduction (Holmes and Redmond 2010), while acknowledging the many disciplines that contribute studies and insights, locates the journal primarily within media and cultural studies.

This conjoined disciplinary field is common – in University administration, research assessment and funding, publishing practices and self-description. Distinguishing between them is obviously possible, but not of great value for celebrity studies: there is much more to the study of celebrity than media studies alone can handle, but ordinary people's main encounters with celebrities and the industry which produces and manages them are mediated ones. My personal predilection is to see cultural studies as the dominant partner. Whether Turner would agree is unclear. In his essay monograph *What's Become of Cultural Studies?* (Turner 2012), he mentions celebrity only once as a 'topic' instanced in a description of the debased (imaginary) introductory course Cultural Studies 101. It does not make the index. Celebrity has though remained prominent in his publications – there are three books and many articles, though none is mentioned in the 2012 monograph.

In an interview with Noel King (2010), Turner was asked about his relationship with another field, Australian Studies, and in a long answer traces how after a period in the early to mid-1990s focused on international work, he became concerned with Australian topics on current affairs, talk-back radio and celebrity: 'they were all very much a critique of media performance from a left political point of view, but it was not a particularly theorized or sophisticated thing' (p. 149). When asked if there is a single theme unifying his work, he acknowledges the formative power of structuralism and then adds 'a continuing commitment to understanding Australian popular culture' (p. 150). Under-standing Australian celebrity is obviously part of this. The preface to the second edition of *Understanding Celebrity* (2013) places the work still as for 'media and cultural studies scholars' and notes the changes in celebrity studies since the first edition as involving the need for 'better understanding of the cultural and political consequences of celebrity's prominence in our media culture' (p. x). I am taking that here as an endorsement of cultural studies' dominance, if not exclusivity.

Turner is not alone in identifying the lacunae in the field, nor are they specific to Australian celebrity studies. Although not apparently responding to him, David Beer and Ruth Penfold-Mounce (2010) analyzed the state of academic study of celebrity noting both the major increase in journal articles since 2002 and the need to find ways to make such study more valued in the academy. They coin the term 'glossy topics' to describe ones like celebrity which, having high public interest but low public value, are used to berate humanities and social sciences as overly concerned with frivolous matters (p. 363). Perhaps implicitly acknowledging this, in the editorial celebrating three years of *Celebrity Studies*, Holmes and Redmond (2013) wrote of their desire to publish more empirical audience studies as evidence of the political consequence of the field (p. 113).

There is considerable irony in seeing celebrity studies emerging from cultural studies, which in its Birmingham School model was founded in a concern with the underprivileged. The core of celebrity is its privilege, its excess of attention and its exhibition of conspicuous consumption. It is promoted and perceived as an opportunity to escape the constraints of class and race, the very constraints studied in their oppressiveness by early cultural studies scholars. Turner's (most recently 2013, p. 156) insistence on the need to do more in celebrity studies than analyse celebrities as texts (most recently 2013, p. 156) leads him not just to again advocate studies of production and 'the current performance of democratic media ideals through the media' (2013, p. 157), but also to admit the need to know more about celebrity–fan relations. The first two of these require national inflections, but the last does not. An Australian fan may feel no relationship with Australian celebrities and aggregate with other fans digitally as part of a global phenomenon. However focusing on the audience for celebrity and what needs and desires of theirs are being exercised in the relation does take us back closer to our cultural studies origins.

Studies of Australian celebrity before 2000

Examining how celebrity was written about in Australian research before *Fame Games* was published means starting with Langer's (1981) highly influential article on television personalities. It was primarily concerned with establishing television's difference from film along axes such as distance/intimacy and familiar/exceptional (p. 363). His personalities are found in both fictional and non-fictional programmes, primarily American or British, though the list of factual programmes is principally Australian. It does not study any individual in any detail, looking instead at the system, its ideological foundations and consequences. Soon after, in a chapter on mass market magazine, *The Australian Women's Weekly*, cultural commentator Humphrey McQueen (1982) wrote about its editor, Ita Buttrose, in ways that are recognizably celebrity-based, mentioning both her work and her private life (pp. 139–142).

Following this, a long-running news story led to the creation of a very different celebrity, Lindy Chamberlain, initially, in Chris Rojek's (2001) term, a celetoid, but now too long lasting an Australian media presence for the term to apply. Two articles on Chamberlain, wrongly convicted of murdering her baby Azaria, published in *Australian Journal of Cultural Studies* (Johnson 1984, Craik 1987) were early contributions to the long sequence of scholarly and popular publications largely in law, feminism and biography examining the related cases and the various national myths the representations drew on.

The first sustained cultural studies work on pre-existing celebrities centred on businessman, Alan Bond, starting with O'Ryan and Shoesmith (1987), tellingly subtitled 'businessmen as stars', and culminating in Turner (1994). Bond was ideal as an exemplar of changes in the popular Australian representation of capitalists in the 1980s, not only because of the heavy media coverage of his takeovers and private life, but also because he led the successful challenge for the America's Cup in 1983, which was a powerful component in 'the alignment between representations of the interests of business and those of the nation' (Turner 1994, p. 23). Although both pieces talk of him as a celebrity and a star and trace elements of his media profile, that is not their purpose; rather the authors discuss how business itself and the markets became aestheticized sites of performance (Turner 1994, pp. 18–19). The America's Cup made it possible for sports sociologist Jim McKay (1991) to contribute to this analysis, though inasmuch as he engaged in celebrity study it was of then Prime Minister Bob Hawke as much as of Bond (pp. 24–29).

Despite being about Federal Treasurer, later Prime Minister, Paul Keating, rather than Bond, Morris (1992) is related to that project. Examining her own reactions to Keating's televised performance speaking about the economy during the late 1980s, in the light of shifts in the representation and practice of economics itself, Morris asserts that more than 'aestheticizing politics, Keating was "eroticizing economics"' (p. 50). Although thoroughly located in Australian data of the early 1990s, it remains both one of the most sophisticated examinations of a fan's response to a celebrity and most powerful contributions to cultural analysis of an economic shift available from any scholar.

Running in parallel with this was Wark's (1988, 1993, 1999) consideration of music and politics looking at singer and politician Peter Garrett. The study of Midnight Oil frontman Garrett, modulated across three appearances all concerning his environmental politics as much as his music. It first appeared (1988) not long after Garrett's failed bid for a Senate seat for the Nuclear Disarmament Party, changed title only for the 1993 collection and was expanded for its 1999 appearance, which predated his shift to the Australian Labour Party, election and subsequent appointment as Minister variously for Environment and School Education. Wark called Garrett an organic intellec-tual, though the essay mainly examined authenticity through distinguishing popular from pre-packaged music. There was no mention of Garrett's private life or his appearance. In the 1999 book, the study comprised part of a larger section on music celebrity with another chapter looking at the international-ization of singers Kylie Minogue and Nick Cave, and an introductory chapter mentioning more domestic musicians, a couple of scandals of the day and a long précis of Marshall's (1997) *Celebrity and Power*. Later sections of the book on Australian Federal politics included a discussion of Paul Keating with elements addressing his celebrity.

John Hartley's (1996) *Popular Reality* considered changes in journalistic practice including much greater personalization and centring discussion around the media treatment of Nelson Mandela and Australian actor, Sophie Lee. Of the works mentioned in this section, this is the first since Langer's *Media Culture and Society* article to have been published neither by an Australian publisher (or the Australian arm of an international one) nor in an Australian journal.

Langer's (1998) *Tabloid Television* included a chapter entitled 'The Especially Remarkable', Langer's second major contribution to the field. Locating himself and the book in media studies and journalism, he conducted a survey of four weeks of news on four Australian television channels to underpin his examination of the 'other news', those 'soft' stories which customarily conclude a bulletin. His discussion of celebrities is determined by their occurrence in his sample and includes international entertainers and members of royalty visiting Australia, as well as the then Australian cricket captain, Graham Yallop, marathoner Tony Rafferty, and actor Reg Livermore. The actual identity of the celebrities is unimportant to his argument, since they are included in a discussion of a distinctive and regularly overlooked type of journalism, rather than being the focus of his analysis. They do however help ground the work, published internationally, as Australian.

A year earlier than that, the Re:Public (1997) collection *Planet Diana* explored the 'Global Mourning' over the death of Princess Diana, focusing both on the popular response and on 'the icon'. Lumby (1999) on changes in the tabloid media in the 1990s targeted both an academic and a (an educated) popular audience. She is concerned quite extensively with celebrity, using international, national and internationally known Australian examples, like model Elle McPherson and actor Nicole Kidman. Both books came from Australian publishers.

I have concentrated on books more than articles here, in part because it was possible to do so for that period more than is now the case, but one of the most thoughtful interventions in the study of celebrity by an Australian was John Frow's (1998) *International Journal of Cultural Studies* examination of Elvis Presley. The value of this piece lies in its outlining a method for cultural analysis of the conjunction of celebrity and religion, a method sadly not adopted in subsequent forays into the conjunction. Frow talked of stars more often than celebrities and while he acknowledged his Australian location, he named no Australian celebrities. Jon Stratton's (1997) study of the art of Brett Whiteley for an Australian journal obviously did, but it is principally concerned with the Australian artist's attitudes to Romanticism. The emphasis on his biography, contextualized politically, and his reputation, move it towards a consideration of his celebrity, though that word is not used.

The dominant characteristic of the work of this period is that the analysis of individual celebrity figures was in the service of more general contentions: about the economy or other aspects of politics, injustice, art appreciation or changes in journalistic practices. Alternatively the focus was on the reactions of consumers of celebrity, whether Morris herself, those who mourned Diana, or who revered Elvis. Overwhelmingly the work was Australian published. Yet even in those few pieces that were not, where non-Australian celebrities were mentioned, they were examined in Australian texts or through their Australian reception. The self-sufficient analysis of celebrity texts that was later to become so common was foreshadowed only by Wark's (1999) discussion of Kylie and Cave.

Fame Games and **Australian celebrities**

It seems not unreasonable to trace part at least of Turner's insistence on attention being paid to the industrial dimension of celebrity to the work done for *Fame Games*, but such work, like the audience studies Holmes and Redmond call for, requires serious funding if it is to have representative rigour, and the 'glossy topic' quality of the field makes attracting this difficult. We were fortunate the Australian Research Council supported our investigation of the celebrity industry from 1997 to 1999. In the final chapter of the book, having demonstrated the major presence of celebrity coverage in the increased role of publicity in Australian media and warned of the limitations of wholesale condemnation or celebration, we noted some important aspects of the consumption of the celebrity commodity. The first was that for most of the audience of celebrity stories, the celebrity is the only commodity being consumed; that there is no follow through to their other cultural products (p. 169). Furthermore even in contemplating the functions of celebrity in identity formation, most consumption of publicity is distracted, diluted and simply not of great moment (pp. 169–170). In this we were in accord with Joke Hermes' (1995) work on the reception of celebrity in Dutch magazines. On the other hand, particular celebrities carry significant meaning for individual consumers and are used by the industry and the audience to convey identifiable values, so the specificity of critique of selected instances remains important (pp. 178).

The survey of celebrity stories across a sample of Australian television and print media conducted in 1997 as the first stage of the *Fame Games* investigation was limited in how much it could claim by the size of the sample and the paucity of earlier data, although a substantial growth in the presence of Australian celebrities compared to 20 years earlier was clear. When looking at the geographic origin of the individuals in those stories, 36 percent of the Australians mentioned had international links of various kinds, Mel Gibson being the example cited there (pp. 17–18). Given that the great majority of Australian celebrities had no element of international recognizability, this indicates an over-representation of stories about those who had. There is nothing odd about this. Figures like Gibson, Nicole Kidman or Michael

Hutchence had celebrity of greater magnitude and thus newsworthiness than, for instance former test cricketer Max Walker or comedian Wendy Harmer, no matter their domestic recognizability. We identified the former grouping as 'national–international' and probably continued their over-representation as examples in the resulting publication, but most of the individuals discussed still had only national celebrity.

Kylie Minogue as celebrity example

The cover of *Fame Games* uses a photograph of Kylie Minogue at London's Madame Tussauds with her arms around her own waxwork figure. It is a very rich image encapsulating many of the themes of the study, both the promotional work celebrities engage in for themselves and other entities and, more implicitly, the creation of the separate persona of the celebrity behind or beside which a 'real' person may exist. Whoever the celebrity depicted – and such pictures are a standard promotional tool for the waxworks attraction – the photograph would have served well, but a study of Australian celebrity required an Australian figure and Kylie had the international (or at least British, given that the book's publisher was Cambridge University Press) recognizability that meant she was ideal. That we actually discussed aspects of the management of her career while she was appearing on the television soap *Neighbours* was probably unimportant to the cover's graphic designers. Kylie is the go-to Australian celebrity more widely. She appears (collaged with Paul Keating) on the cover of Wark (1999) and is discussed inside, Lumby (1999) considers her more briefly, but Hartley (1996) uses her across three chapters (though Nicole Kidman appears on his cover). The only essay in Philip Hayward's (1992) collection *From Pop to Punk to Postmodernism* to provide a scholarly analysis of a celebrity was Idena Rex (1992) talking of Kylie.

It may be that referring to Kylie in non-condemnatory ways is a distinguishing feature of Australian cultural, and subsequently celebrity, studies. Her usefulness may be diminishing, though; the three references to her in the first edition of *Understanding Celebrity* are reduced to one for the 2013 version and there have been few studies since those occasioned by her breast cancer (see e.g. Bonner and McKay 2006). John Carroll (2010) mentions her as an instance of the 'sneering condescension' with which celebrities may be treated, though leaving unclear whether he too is sneering (p. 489). Celebrity scholars from other countries do not discuss her very often at all. She is referenced occasionally in scholarly writing on popular music, usually in unfavourable terms. British academic Helen Davies (2001) uses her in an analysis of the dismissive treatment of female performers in the British musical press. On a personal note, when I was writing a chapter for the (UK) Open University text *Understanding Media: Inside Celebrity* (Bonner 2005) I had to fight the course team to use her rather than yet another (American) male singer as an example. There was no similar complaint about my inclusion of Kidman or the Australian cricket team.

The impact of changes in publishing practices

I have already indicated that Australian book length works discussing celebrity were more common before than after 2000. In part this is a consequence of changes in publishing practices. Several publishers producing cultural studies-related material ceased operation, others narrowed their lists substantially, while yet others closed their Australian branches. Australian scholars now have few local publishing options for monographs or collections. Morris (2006) describes the situation accurately as one where international publishing consortia pressure 'Australian critics who seek an academic base to sell their work in the first instance to trans-Atlantic readers *as a condition* of its publication and thus, in the fullness of time, its distribution to Australians' (p. 4, her emphasis). The wider readership international English-language publication brings is accompanied by the potential for a commensurate reputation but at the expense of a fully Australian focus. Editors all too often ask for, at the least, comparative American material and authors quickly learn to exemplify their argument's claims with celebrities drawn from Hollywood's A-list or sporting or musical equivalents.

It did not happen abruptly as the millennium arrived; two books closer to the precursor publications in cultural studies demonstrate the transition. Susan Hopkins' (2002) *Girl Heroes* examines the Girl Power phenomenon in the wake of the success of the Spice Girls, though drawing more on women's studies than celebrity frameworks. Publisher, Pluto Press Australia, categorized it as 'Feminist Studies/Popular Culture'. While it draws on many international examples, it is solidly located as an Australian work, calling on Australian television and magazines and referencing national and national–international celebrities (including Kylie) substantially. Toby Miller's (2001) *Sportsex* from an American academic publisher, but by a then long-term American-resident Australian, argues optimistically that changed attitudes to gender and sexuality were observable in Australian and American sporting celebrities.

The paucity of Australian monographs subsequently has occurred at a time of considerable growth in the numbers of relevant journals internationally. Although a couple of these have an Austral(as)ian focus, some local ones have moved offshore or folded, so there has not been much increase in Australian located and edited outlets. Continuity is provided by *Media International Australia* and *Cultural Studies Review*, for which celebrity is only occasionally a topic, as well as by *Continuum* and the *Journal of Australian Studies* that have both more often carried relevant articles. While *Continuum* has always been editorially located in Australia, it publishes much with neither content nor authorial connection to the country, though still more with such connections than journals located offshore. The *Journal of Australian Studies* has carried many articles on famous Australians in both of the periods considered here. The majority is of historical figures and employ historical methods, but 'celebrity' is more likely to appear in the title of articles published after 2000, as it does for Jacqueline Zara Wilson's (2004) study of Chopper Read and dark tourism.

A potentially hospitable recent addition is the *Australasian Journal of Popular Culture*. Of the eight issues published at the time of writing only three articles had concerned celebrities, none were by Australian academics or about Australian celebrities. Lindsay Neill and Claudia Bell's (2013) fine examination of New Zealand celebrities in stories promoting pie carts (mobile food vendors) in the period 1950–1970 is similar to material carried in *Journal of Australian Studies*.

It is understandable, but the practice of Australian scholars writing on internationally recognizable celebrities, including ones with no Australian connection, rather than ones familiar only to Australians has intensified in the recent period. The number of international journals carrying articles by Australian scholars or (less commonly) on Australian celebrities means that the survey that follows is necessarily selective, although particular attention has been paid to journals editorially located in Australia, especially those mentioned above.

This is not solely an Australian problem, but shared with others outside the English-language publishing centres of the UK and USA. Wanting to write on celebrities lacking recognition beyond the home nation becomes even more problematic for smaller geographic areas. Ruth McElroy and Rebecca Williams (2011) coin the term 'localebrity' (p. 190) and explore its implications in a study considering reality television participants on a programme screened only in Wales. Olivier Driessens (2012) has conducted extensive research on celebrity in the Flemish-speaking part of Belgium. At the 2012 International Celebrity Studies conference in Melbourne, he sensibly chose to speak about the methodological implications of his work rather than its case studies. The burden of his argument was the importance of interviewing the celebrities themselves, which chimed with McElroy and Williams' practice and showed an advantage of small locations. Access to localebrities is easier to obtain than to those of greater magnitude. Difficulties of access mean that almost all celebrity studies scholars in major English-speaking countries have drawn their material for analysis from celebrity news and profiles.

Australian studies of celebrity post-2000

Fame Games was thoroughly located in the Australian situation. Comparisons with the UK and USA were made, but the national specificity of the industry examined was the primary concern. Only as a consequence of providing the Australian data were wider claims about celebrity made. The book thus differs substantially from Turner's subsequent solo celebrity publications where celebrity is considered as a global phenomenon and the overwhelming majority of celebrities instanced have international fame. Eight Australian celebrities and one pop group are mentioned in each edition of *Understanding Celebrity* (2004 and 2013), six and the pop group recur; Dannii Minogue and Nicole Kidman are only in the first edition, while Cate Blanchett and Peter Garrett are added for the second. With the exception of the two actors just mentioned, Kylie Minogue and possibly comedian Barry Humphries/Dame Edna Everage, the Australians mentioned need the explanatory introductions for a non-Australian readership to understand the points they are illustrating. *Understanding Celebrity* is aimed at an international market by an international publisher; it is located in Australian celebrity studies only because Turner is its pre-eminent practitioner.

The other major relevant monograph from an international publisher is Redmond's (2014) *Celebrity and the Media*, targeted, like Turner (2004, 2013) at the international textbook market. It takes a distinctively idiosyncratic approach, valuably concerning itself substantially with the emotional content of audience engagement with celebrities. Most examples are American, with British second and also a couple of Asian references. Only two Australia celebrities receive extended consideration: national–international Cate Blanchett, whose work promoting skincare brand SK-II allows a discussion of whiteness (pp. 58–62) and Charlotte Dawson, not an international name, demonstrating the damage celebrity trolling can do (p. 105). (This latter has become more powerful since the time of writing, following Dawson's 2014 suicide.) A few other national–international Australian examples, including Kylie, are mentioned in passing.

My (necessarily selective) article survey reveals that while it is not essential to use non-Australian or national–international celebrities to be published internationally, it is common to call on them both there and in nationally located sites. Even in instances where the celebrity is non-Australian, it is very rare for the Australian context of a study to be disavowed completely. Most commonly, as with Jeanette Delamoir's (2008) discussion of star bodies concentrating on Renée Zellweger, by drawing on Australian source material, here through her Australian magazine coverage. Patsy McCarthy and Caroline Hatcher's (2005) analysis of Richard Branson as a celebrity entrepreneur only briefly acknowledges his operations in Australia, but uses Australian newspapers for primary data.

Sometimes there is a more complicated approach. In the endnote to an essay on literary celebrity for the Redmond and Holmes *Reader*, Wenche Ommundsen (2007) acknowledged support for the project underpinning it and added, as if in apology: 'A number of illustrations given in this paper reflect the specifically Australian focus of its empirical research, though most, we argue, are indicative of trends in public literary culture world-wide' (p. 254). Even so, Salman Rushdie is her principal example and the (primarily non-pictorial) 'illustrations' were of writers' festivals and other literary promotions. With the single exception of the non-celebrity Australian author Rosie Scott, all other writers named in the piece were British and the non-literary celebrities British or American.

The first two instances of national–international celebrity use come from *Continuum*, as noted above pitched more internationally than most other Australian located journals. Tania Lewis' (2001) examination of the contemporary celebrity intellectual looks at Australian-born art critic Robert Hughes starting with the reception of his television programme *Beyond the Fatal Shore* in Australia (bad) compared to the USA and UK (good). It thus uses a (then) internationally recognizable figure to make a global case but against a decisively Australian setting.

Katrina Jaworski's (2008) examination of gendered representations of suicide is centred on the deaths of Michael Hutchence and Paula Yates. She uses Australian newspaper coverage as primary evidence. Internationally known Australian singer Hutchence anchors the article, its title and the analytic use of spectacle, even though more space is devoted to British celebrity Yates, whose accidental death/suicide carries the weight of the gender argument.

The next might be seen as a special case, since, while *Social Semiotics* has been editorially located in the UK since 2002, it began as Australian. Felicity Collins' (2008) study of 'ethical violence' discusses Russell Crowe in an (Australian) chat show and indigenous actor David Gulpilil in a documentary, acknowledging her choice to be of 'internationalized' Australians (p. 194). She argues that these instances provide opportunities for both celebrities to reject conservative depictions of, respectively, Crowe's Australian masculinity and Gulpilil's 'divided' Aboriginality (pp. 198–199). The close attention to Australianness through the particularities of the two celebrities, the texts in which they appear and the time of screening complicates the view of the identity work celebrities perform discussed in other analyses.

That it is possible to publish national material in an international journal is evidenced by Brent McDonald and Daniel Eagles' (2012) examination of Australian diver Matthew Mitcham as a gay sporting icon, and by Jason Wilson's (2011) brief item on celebrity and Australian Prime Minister Kevin Rudd. Both appear in *Celebrity Studies* (the first in a special Olympics issue) which could be argued to be more understanding of an Australian viewpoint given the co-editorship of Sean Redmond and the status of Australian celebrity scholars generally. That does not apply to *Media, Culture and Society* where Jason Bainbridge and Jane Bestwick's (2010) study of celebrity presenters appeared. It is based in an empirical study of Australian newsreading, but draws on American comparisons to make internationally relevant points. In comparison, Bainbridge's (2009) solo article in an Australian journal is centred on national reporting of a local mining disaster. My own study (Bonner 2007) of a local lifestyle and fashion celebrity appeared in the resolutely national *Australian Cultural History*.

The survey reveals that Australianness is most evident in the source of the data drawn on rather than the celebrity's nationality or the journal's location, though all are significant.

An alternate way of making Australian celebrities internationally 'legible' is to analyze local versions of international television formats. Charles Fairchild (2006, 2008) looks at *Idol*, while Robert Payne's (2009) study of the performance of masculinity by Australian celebrities Tom Williams and Jake Wall examines local versions of *Dancing with the Stars* and *Dancing on Ice*. A variant considers an Australian programme sold offshore, as is the case with Julia Eberhart's (2013, 2014) work on the reception of the shows of Australian comedian Chris Lilley.

The Australian celebrity most discussed in the literature for this period was Steve Irwin. In contrast to the Australian cultural and celebrity studies use of Kylie as an internationally recognizable referent, examinations of Irwin's celebrity, embodiment of Australian national identity and role in the growth of the action-adventure-hero presenter in natural history television, are mainly written by non-Australian residents (Chris 2006, Rayner 2007, Brockington 2008, Brown 2010). Australian environmental researchers Jesse K. Northfield and Clive R. McMahon's (2010) argument that he functioned as an environmental celebrity is actually a riposte to Brown's article on reactions to Irwin's death naming him a conservation hero. The only major Australian piece, Folker Hanusch's (2009) examination of commemorative journalism through the coverage of Irwin's death approaches a celebrity study through considering the media's role in mythologizing him. The comparative silence by Australian scholars in conjunction with the atypical non-Australian interest leaves this an anomalous situation in Australian celebrity studies.

Conclusion

One of the problems posed for an analysis of the state of Australian celebrity studies is that so many of its researchers, most notably Turner, Marshall and Redmond, are leading international scholars in the field. They publish and speak internationally, do not disavow their nationality, but rarely use national examples. Even when they do, the point is rarely to talk of national concerns. Marshall (2010) devotes equal space to Tiger Woods and Australian yachts-woman Jessica Watson, but this continues his arguments about the (celebrity) cultural shifts occasioned by social media. It is not more about Australia through Watson, than it is about the USA through Woods. In conjunction with the publishing changes which have led to fewer local monographs and more scholars publishing internationally on internationally recognizable celebrities, the existence of Australian celebrity studies cannot be regarded as secure.

This need not be entirely deplored. Celebrity itself is more transnational, and not just through American dominance. Australians of varied ethnic backgrounds follow K-pop and J-pop celebrities, Bollywood stars and European or Latin American footballers. Our cultural studies' heritage though properly requires us to pay attention to context. Turner's own work on the continuing significance of the national in television studies (see e.g. Turner and Tay 2009) should inform celebrity studies too. Transnational and international celebrity does not eradicate distinctive national manifestations and they need to be investigated, especially by people familiar with the culture in which they exist.

This article has examined whether one of the things that has happened to Australian cultural studies was the fracturing off from it of a sub-discipline of Australian celebrity studies, with a concomitant effect that some scholars who would once have contributed to the parent field now have another focus. The answer is far from clear-cut. Studies of Australian celebrities emerged in and from Australian cultural studies, as did Australian scholars of celebrity, but it is hard to identify distinctively Australian celebrity studies post-2000. Few if any Australian scholars sustain a career solely focusing on celebrity, but quite a few spend time writing on it. Yet the integration of celebrity into a broader analysis of Australian culture that characterized the earlier period is certainly less evident. We do not 'do' celebrity distinctively here now – or if we do, scholars are not paying attention to it.

Disclosure statement

No potential conflict of interest was reported by the author.

References

Alberoni, F. (1962) '"The powerless elite": theory and sociological research on the phenomenon of the stars', in *Sociology of Mass Communication*, ed. D. McQuail, London, Penguin Books, pp. 75–98.
Bainbridge, J. (2009) 'Going down the hole: the reporting of the Beaconsfield mine disaster', *Cultural Studies Review*, vol. 15, no. 1, pp. 43–64.

Bainbridge, J. & Bestwick, J. (2010) '"And here's the news": analyzing the evolution of the marketed newsreader', *Media, Culture and Society*, vol. 32, no. 2, pp. 1–19.

Beer, D. & Penfold-Mounce, R. (2010) 'Researching glossy topics: the case of the academic study of celebrity', *Celebrity Studies*, vol. 1, no. 3, pp. 360–365.

Bonner, F. (2005) 'The celebrity in the text', in *Understanding Media: Inside Celebrity*, eds. J. Evans & D. Hesmondhalgh, Maidenhead, Open University Press, pp. 57–96.

Bonner, F. (2007) 'A familiar face: the consequences of a long career on-screen', *Australian Cultural History*, vol. 26, pp. 91–112.

Bonner, F. & McKay, S. (2006) 'The illness narrative: Australian media reporting of Kylie Minogue's breast cancer', *Metro*, vol. 148, pp. 154–159.

Boorstin, D. J. (1987/1962) *The Image: A Guide to Pseudo-events in America*, New York, Vintage Books.

Boorstin, D. J. (2006/1961) 'From hero to celebrity: the human pseudo-event', in *The Celebrity Culture Reader*, ed. P. D. Marshall, London, Routledge, pp. 72–90.

Braudy, L. (1986) *The Frenzy of Renown: Fame and Its History*, New York, Oxford University Press.

Brockington, D. (2008) 'Celebrity conservation: interpreting the Irwins', *Media International Australia, Incorporating Culture and Policy*, vol. 127, pp. 96–108.

Brown, W. J. (2010) 'Steve Irwin's influence on wildlife conservation', *Journal of Communication*, vol. 60, no. 1, pp. 73–93.

Carroll, J. (2010) 'The tragicomedy of celebrity', *Society*, vol. 47, no. 6, pp. 489–492.

Chris, C. (2006) *Watching Wildlife*, Minneapolis, University of Minnesota Press.

Collins, F. (2008) 'The ethical violence of celebrity chat: Russell Crowe and David Gulpilil', *Social Semiotics*, vol. 18, no. 2, pp. 191–204.

Craik, J. (1987) 'The Azaria Chamberlain case: a question of infanticide', *Australian Journal of Cultural Studies*, vol. 4, no. 2, pp. 120–151.

Davies, H. (2001) 'All rock and roll is homosocial: the representation of women in the British rock music press', *Popular Music*, vol. 20, no. 3, pp. 301–319.

Delamoir, J. (2008) 'Star bodies/freak bodies/women's bodies', *Media International Australia*, vol. 127, pp. 44–56.

Driessens, O. (2012) 'Where are the agents in celebrity studies research? Some considerations on interviewing celebrities', paper presented at the *Inaugural Celebrity Studies Conference*, Deakin University, Melbourne, 12–14 December.

Dyer, R. (1979) *Stars*, London, BFI.

Eberhart, J. (2013) '"Your heart goes out to the Australian Tourist Board": critical uncertainty and the management of censure in Chris Lilley's TV comedies', *Continuum: Journal of Media and Cultural Studies*, vol. 27, no. 3, pp. 434–445.

Eberhart, J. (2014) '"Mr G is deffinately bringin' sexy back": characterising Chris Lilley's YouTube audience', *Continuum: Journal of Media and Cultural Studies*, vol. 28, no. 2, pp. 176–187.

Fairchild, C. (2006) '*Australian Idol* and the attention economy', in *The Celebrity Culture Reader*, ed. P. D Marshall, London, Routledge, pp. 286–290.

Fairchild, C. (2008) *Pop Idols and Pirates: Mechanisms of Consumption and Global Circulation*, Aldershot, Ashgate.

Frow, J. (1998) 'Is Elvis a god? Cult, culture, questions of method', *International Journal of Cultural Studies*, vol. 1, no. 2, pp. 197–210.

Gamson, J. (1994) *Claims to Fame: Celebrity in Contemporary America*, Berkeley, University of California Press.

Hanusch, F. (2009) '"The Australian we all aspire to be": commemorative journalism and the death of the crocodile hunter', *Media International Australia*, vol. 130, pp. 28–38.

Hartley, J. (1996) *Popular Reality: Journalism, Modernity, Popular Culture*, London, Arnold.

Hayward, P. (ed.) (1992) *From Pop to Punk to Postmodernism: Popular Music and Australian Culture from the 1960s to the 1990s*, North Sydney, Allen & Unwin.

Hermes, J. (1995) *Reading Women's Magazines: An Analysis of Everyday Media Use*, Cambridge, Polity Press.

Holmes, S. & Redmond, S. (2010) 'Editorial: a journal in *Celebrity Studies*', *Celebrity Studies*, vol. 1, no. 1, pp. 1–10.

Holmes, S. & Redmond, S. (2013) 'Introduction: *Celebrity studies* in rude health', *Celebrity Studies*, vol. 4, no. 2, pp. 113–114.

Hopkins, S. (2002) *Girl Heroes: The New Force in Popular Culture*, Annandale, Pluto Press Australia.

Jaworski, K. (2008) '"Elegantly wasted": the celebrity deaths of Michael Hutchence and Paula Yates', *Continuum: Journal of Media and Cultural Studies*, vol. 22, no. 6, pp. 777–791.

Johnson, D. (1984) 'From fairy to witch: imagery as myth in the Azaria case', *Australian Journal of Cultural Studies*, vol. 2, no. 2, pp. 90–106.

King, N. (2010) 'Interview with Professor Graeme Turner, November 9, 2007', *Television and New Media*, vol. 11, no. 2, pp. 143–156.

Langer, J. (1981) 'Television's "personality system"', *Media Culture and Society*, vol. 3, no. 4, pp. 351–365. (Reprinted in Marshall 2006).

Langer, J. (1998) *Tabloid Television: Popular Journalism and the 'Other News'*, London, Routledge.

Lewis, T. (2001) 'Embodied experts: Robert Hughes, cultural studies and the celebrity intellectual', *Continuum: Journal of Media and Cultural Studies*, vol. 15, no. 2, pp. 233–247.

Lumby, C. (1999) *Gotcha: Life in a Tabloid World*, St Leonards, Allen & Unwin.

Marshall, P. D. (1997) *Celebrity and Power: Fame in Contemporary Culture*, Minneapolis, Minnesota University Press.

Marshall, P. D. (ed.) (2006) *The Celebrity Culture Reader*, London, Routledge.

Marshall, P. D. (2010) 'The specular economy', *Society*, vol. 47, pp. 498–502.

McCarthy, P. & Hatcher, C. (2005) 'Branding Branson: a case study of a celebrity entrepreneur', *Australian Journal of Communication*, vol. 32, no. 3, pp. 45–61.

McDonald, B. & Eagles, D. (2012) 'Matthew Mitcham: the narrative of a gay sporting icon', *Celebrity Studies*, vol. 3, no. 3, pp. 297–318.

McElroy, R. & Williams, R. (2011) 'Remembering ourselves, viewing the others: historical reality television and celebrity in the small nation', *Television and New Media*, vol. 12, no. 3, pp. 187–206.

McKay, J. (1991) *No Pain, No Gain? Sport and Australian Culture*, Sydney, Prentice Hall of Australia.

McQueen, H. (1982) *Gone Tomorrow: Australia in the 80s*, Sydney, Angus & Robertson.

Miller, T. (2001) *Sportsex*, Philadelphia, PA, Temple University Press.

Morris, M. (1992) *Ecstasy and Economics: American Essays for John Forbes*, Rose Bay, Empress.

Morris, M. (2006) *Identity Anecdotes: Translation and Media Culture*, London, Sage.

Neill, L. & Bell, C. (2013) 'Negotiating change: celebrity pie cart narratives', *Australasian Journal of Popular Culture*, vol. 2, no. 1, pp. 93–105.

Northfield, J. K. & McMahon, C. R. (2010) 'Crikey! Overstating the conservation influence of the crocodile hunter', *Science Communication*, vol. 32, no. 3, pp. 412–417.

Ommundsen, W. (2007) 'From the altar to the market-place and back again: understanding literary celebrity', in *Stardom and Celebrity: A Reader*, eds. S. Redmond & S. Holmes, London, Sage, pp. 244–255.

O'Ryan, G. & Shoesmith, B. (1987) 'Speculation, promise and performance: businessmen as stars', *Australian Journal of Cultural Studies*, vol. 4, no. 2, pp. 163–173.

Payne, R. (2009) 'Dancing with the ordinary: masculine celebrity performance on Australian TV', *Continuum: Journal of Media and Cultural Studies*, vol. 23, no. 3, pp. 295–306.

Rayner, J. (2007) 'Live and dangerous? The screen life of Steve Irwin', *Studies in Australasian Cinema*, vol. 1, no. 1, pp. 107–117.

Re:Public (ed.) (1997) *Planet Diana: Cultural Studies and Global Mourning*, Sydney, Research Centre in Intercommunal Studies, University of Western Sydney.

Redmond, S. (2014) *Celebrity and the Media*, London, Palgrave Macmillan.

Redmond, S. & Holmes, S. (eds.) (2007) *Stardom and Celebrity: A Reader*, London, Sage.

Rex, I. (1992) 'Kylie: the making of a star', in *From Pop to Punk to Postmodernism: Popular Music and Australian Culture from the 1960s to the 1990s*, ed. P. Hayward, North Sydney, Allen & Unwin, pp. 149–159.

Rojek, C. (2001) *Celebrity*, London, Reaktion Books.

Stratton, J. (1997) 'Brett Whiteley: the last Australian romantic', *The UTS Review*, vol. 3, no. 1, pp. 183–207.

Turner, G. (1992) 'Of rocks and hard places: the colonized, the national and Australian Cultural Studies', *Cultural Studies*, vol. 6, no. 3, pp. 424–432.

Turner, G. (1994) *Making It National: Nationalism and Australian Popular Culture*, St Leonards, Allen & Unwin.

Turner, G. (2004) *Understanding Celebrity*, London, Sage.

Turner, G. (2010) 'Approaching cultural studies', *Celebrity Studies*, vol. 1, no. 1, pp. 11–21.

Turner, G. (2012) *What's Become of Cultural Studies?* London, Sage.

Turner, G. (2013) *Understanding Celebrity*, 2nd edn, London, Sage.

Turner, G., Bonner, F. & Marshall, P. D. (2000) *Fame Games: The Production of Celebrity in Australia*, Melbourne, Cambridge University Press.

Turner, G. & Tay, J. (eds.) (2009) *Television Studies after TV: Understanding Television in the Post-broadcast Era*, London, Routledge.

Wark, M. (1988) 'Homage to catatonia: the rise and rise of Peter Garrett', *Meanjin*, vol. 47, no. 2, pp. 298–309.

Wark, M. (1993) 'Homage to catatonia: culture, politics and Midnight Oil', in *Australian Cultural Studies: A Reader*, eds. J. Frow & M. Morris, St Leonards, Allen & Unwin, pp. 105–116.

Wark, M. (1999) *Celebrities, Culture and Cyberspace: The Light on the Hill in a Postmodern World*, Annandale, Pluto Press Australia.

Weber, M. (2006/1922) 'The sociology of charismatic authority; The nature of charismatic authority and its routinization', in *The Celebrity Culture Reader*, ed. D. Marshall, London, Routledge, pp. 55–71.

Wilson, J. (2011) 'Sunrise to sunset: Kevin Rudd as celebrity in Australia's post-broadcast democracy', *Celebrity Studies*, vol. 2, no. 1, pp. 97–99.

Wilson, J. Z. (2004) 'Dark tourism and the celebrity prisoner: front and back regions in representations of an Australian historical prison', *Journal of Australian Studies*, vol. 28, no. 82, pp. 1–13.

Tony Bennett

CULTURAL STUDIES AND THE CULTURE CONCEPT

My purpose in this paper is to complicate the genealogies of the concept of culture as a way of life that have held sway within cultural studies. I do so by reviewing key aspects in the development of this concept within the 'Americanist' tradition of anthropology pioneered by Franz Boas in the opening decades of the twentieth century and continued by a generation of Boas's students including Ruth Benedict, Alfred Kroeber and Margaret Mead. I focus on three issues: the respects in which the 'culture concept' was shaped by aesthetic conceptions of form; its spatial registers; and its functioning as a new surface of government, partially displacing that of race, in the development of American multicultural policies in the 1920s and 1930s. In relating these concerns to Graeme Turner's enduring interest in the processes through which culture is 'made national', I indicate how the spatial registers of the culture concept anticipate contemporary approaches to these questions. I also outline what Australian cultural studies has to learn from the American evolution of the culture concept in view of the respects in which the latter was shaped by the racial dynamics of a 'settler' society during a period of heightened immigration from new sources. In concluding, I review the broader implications of the fusion of aesthetic and anthropological forms of expertise that informed the development of the culture concept.

There is little doubt that the concept of culture as a way of life initially provided the key authorizing concept for cultural studies as a distinctive intellectual and political practice. In endorsing Williams's definition, in *The Long Revolution*, of 'the theory of culture as the study of relationships between elements in a whole way of life' (Williams cit. CCCS 2013, p. 884), the authors of the Fifth Report of the Birmingham Centre for Contemporary Cultural Studies identify three distinctive aspects of culture so defined: first, it interprets culture as 'the whole pattern or configuration of values and meanings in a society'; second, it includes all forms of culture, whether 'high', 'popular' or 'low'; and third, it views these expressive forms as an integral part of social life (CCCS 2013, p. 883). Yet the cultural studies literature has paid scant attention to either the distinctive intellectual qualities this concept acquired or the uses to which it was put in the ongoing process of refashioning that characterized its anthropological interpretation in America during the second, third and fourth decades of the twentieth century. Instead, following Williams's discussion in *Keywords* (Williams 1976) and elsewhere,[1] it has rarely gone any further than to reference Edward Burnett Tylor's conception of culture as 'taken in its wide ethnographic sense ... that complex whole which includes knowledge, belief, art, morals, law, custom, and any other capabilities and habits acquired by man as a member of society' (Tylor 1871, p. 1). This has also typically been evoked as an alternative to the evaluative hierarchies of aesthetic conceptions of culture. Considered assessments of the subsequent development of the concept within what is, for good reasons,[2] pointedly referred to as 'Americanist' anthropology have been notably lacking.[3]

This is both surprising and regrettable. It is surprising in that many of the early formulations of cultural studies owe a good deal more to the intellectual legacy of the post-Boasian trajectories of the culture concept than they do to Tylor. The reference in the Birmingham Centre annual report to 'the whole pattern of configuration of values and meanings' thus reflects the principles of the 'configurational anthropology' that Benedict introduced in her *Patterns of Culture*.[4] Williams also picks up on this aspect of Benedict's discussion when, in *The Long Revolution*, he says that 'it is with the discovery of patterns of a characteristic kind that any useful cultural analysis begins' (Williams 1965, p. 63). These perspectives formed a part of the intellectual milieu from which cultural studies emerged owing to the impact that American anthropology had on British debates about, and practical engagements with, culture in the 1930s and 1940s, particularly through Mass Observation.[5] The culture concept also shaped early American engagements with the analysis of mainstream American culture and its various subcultures – the R. Lynd and H. M. Lynd (1929) study of Middletown, William Whyte's study of street-corner gang life (Whyte 1993) and John Dollard's study of the relations between caste and class (Dollard 1957), for example, which, in turn, significantly influenced CCCS's early work on subcultures (see Hall and Jefferson 1975).

The neglect is regrettable for a number of reasons. Overlooking the twentieth-century history of the concept to claim, in Tylor, the conceptual foundations for a radical intellectual project is scarcely credible. Critical examinations of Tylor's concept have made clear its connections with Eurocentric cultural hierarchies, evolutionary conceptions of racial difference and genocidal colonial projects (Stocking 1968, Bennett 1998, Wolfe 1999). The failure to disentangle the Boasian and post-Boasian development of the culture concept from Tylor's version has also meant that the more instructive lessons that this tradition has to offer cultural studies have not been articulated. Fortunately, though, in the process of abandoning it, American anthropologists have conducted a prolonged critical engagement with the American history of the culture concept, sometimes reflecting on its relations to the currency of culture as a way of life in British cultural studies.[6] The concept has been similarly probed by post-structuralist tendencies in American literary studies.[7] My purpose, in drawing on these literatures, though, is not to propose the culture concept as a model for cultural studies. There are, as we will see, good reasons why the concept fell out of favour within American anthropology, and no point is served by proposing its rehabilitation. I want rather to qualify and complicate how cultural studies has viewed its relations to its conceptual 'pre-history' and to identify some of the implications of this for its work in the present.

There will be three main aspects to my argument. First, I shall show that, far from offering an alternative to aesthetic conceptions of culture, the American culture concept was inherently aesthetic in its constitution. There is now a considerable literature exploring how Williams, in connecting the concept of culture as a way of life to the analysis of class relations, translated post-Kantian aesthetic conceptions into the politico-aesthetic project of the creation of a common culture – some of it favourable (Eagleton 2000) and some more critical (Hunter 1988). The aesthetic registers of the Boasian culture concept are different, focused more on the relations between race, nation and culture, but equally consequential. Second, I shall review Boasian accounts of the relationships between processes of diffusion and the organization of culture areas for the light they throw on the relations between space and cultural flows in ways that anticipated some the contemporary debates concerning the relations between culture, nation, globalization and processes of hybridization. Third, I shall argue that it was precisely the relations between the concept's aesthetic and spatial qualities that informed the concept's governmental deployment, in 1920s and 1930s America, as a resource for managing the relations between America's white 'nativist' stock and new generations of immigrants. This registered a departure from, while still remaining in the slipstream of, the earlier functioning of racial categories as the key means of managing the relations between different generations of immigrants and both Native Americans and African-Americans.

I shall, in addressing these concerns, relate them to Graeme Turner's ongoing engagement with the dynamics of Australian national cultural formation as perhaps the most enduring signature of his work. This is signalled by the titles of many of the books that he has written, co-authored or edited – *Making it National: Nationalism and Australian Popular Culture* (1994); *National Fictions: Literature, Film and the Construction of Australian Narrative* (1986); *Myths of Oz: Reading Australian Popular Culture* (1987); *Nation, Culture, Text: Australian Cultural and Media Studies* (1993) – but is also present in other work: his recent studies of television, for example (Turner and Pertierra 2013). Taken as a whole, his oeuvre offers a sustained intervention into debates concerning the distinguishing qualities of a national culture which, in its scope and depth, has no parallel in the cultural studies literature. Ranging widely across music, painting, film, television, literature, museums, exhibitions and everyday practices, Turner's historical canvass has stretched over the period from the occupation of Australia to the nationing projects of the post-Federation period, while also offering a closer examination of the changes that have characterized the 'postcolonial' projects of the post-war period.[8] Breaker Morant, Yothu Yindi, Marcus Clarke, the bicentennial celebrations of 1988, the Australian pub, Crocodile Dundee, the Heidelberg school, Tom Roberts, Jack Thompson, Peter Carey, *Strictly Ballroom*, John Laws and talkback radio, Alan Bond and the business sector, Malcolm Turnbull and republicanism: these are just some of the key figures, moments, texts and genres that Turner has discussed, placing them in the context of the changing coordinates of gender, class, ethnicity, sexuality and indigeneity that have shaped, and been shaped by, the dynamics of Australian culture.

Turner has also probed the distinctive qualities of Australian cultural studies by placing its approach to the relations between culture and nation in a comparative perspective. In his introduction to *Nation, Culture, Text*, he argues that 'living in a new country' involves 'constant encounters with, and definite possibilities for intervening in, an especially explicit, mutable but insistent, process of nation formation'. This is contrasted to British cultural studies in which '"Britain" is exnominated; it is the unquestioned category which needs never to be spoken', and to American cultural studies which Turner sees as steering clear of such questions given the tendency for 'the American nation [to be] ritually spoken of in order to universalise itself – to, as it were, normatively Americanise the world' (Turner 1993, pp. 8–9). He also suggests that Australian cultural studies exhibits a greater degree of hybridity than these more hegemonic national traditions, melding a wide range of theoretical traditions into a distinctive national theoretical formation shaped by the locally specific challenges of Australian conditions.[9] However, he sees these challenges as being more akin to American nation-culture formations than to British ones. Whereas Australia 'has obsessively defined itself in opposition to Britain', Turner argues, 'its relation to America has largely been constructed in terms of similarity' (Turner 1994, p. 95).

What he has in mind here largely concerns the repertoires of the Australian film and television industries. Yet, at least initially, the dynamics of Australian cultural studies were shaped more by Australian inflections of the class registers that typified British interpretations of the concept of culture as a way of life than by any direct engagement with the American tradition.[10] I want, then, to bend the stick in the other direction by exploring the processes involved in adjusting an imported concept of culture to the task of shaping a national culture that was to be defined against the elitist credentials of European humanist culture. From its initial application in studying the ways of life of Native Americans, the culture concept was subsequently applied in a search for a set of defining values that would distinguish American culture by finding these amidst the ordinary, everyday lives of regular Americans. Moreover, as a concept that was forged by a settler society to negotiate a new set of historical relations between a white north European 'nativist' stock, a radically depleted Native American population, an emancipated African-American population, and new immigrant populations from southern Europe, the American history of the culture concept also speaks directly to the roles that culture has played in Australia's post-war trajectories.

The aesthetic ordering of culture and the authorization of anthropological expertise

Let me go back to Williams who, in his *Keywords* entry on Culture, relies a good deal on *Culture: A Critical Review of Concepts and Definitions* written by two Boasian anthropologists, Alfred Kroeber and Clyde Kluckhohn. The purpose of this survey was to disconnect the anthropological concept of culture from earlier European and humanistic traditions in order to place the study of culture on a purely scientific and American footing. Kroeber and Kluckhohn see this tendency as having had to struggle in face of the more established power of aesthetically evaluative European traditions. They thus note that although Matthew Arnold's *Culture and Anarchy* was published only two years before Tylor's *Primitive Culture*, Arnold's definition of culture as the source of all sweetness and light was recognized by the Oxford English Dictionary in 1893 whereas Tylor's usage had to wait until 1933 for its lexical validation. Their comments on T.S. Eliot have a similar edge to them. Eliot is congratulated for speaking of culture 'in the quite concrete denotation of certain anthropologists' (Kroeber and Kluckhohn 1952, p. 32) as exemplified by his famous characterization of the activities that go together to make up the English way of life. But Kroeber and Kluckhohn take issue with Eliot's elitism – nicely satirized by Williams's characterization of Eliot's list as 'sport, food, a little art' (cit. Eagleton 2000, p. 113) in which the orchestrating principles of English culture (Derby Day, Henley Regatta, Cowes, the 12th of August) had clear ruling-class associations. Eliot is also taken to task for attempting to reconcile 'the humanistic and social science views' (Kroeber and Kluckhohn 1952, p. 33) of culture as a misuse of the American anthropological tradition on which he drew.

Williams is critical of this aspect of Kroeber and Kluckhohn's discussion, insisting that the aesthetic and anthropological uses of the concept cannot be so easily disentangled. This bears crucially on their contention that Tyler's 1871 definition of culture and Boas's culture concept constituted the two key milestones on the royal road to the science they wished to establish. For in clasping Tylor and Boas together, they neglected the differences between them. These particularly concern the Boasian sense of culture as a creatively ordered whole in which the elements which comprise it are configured into a distinctively patterned way of life. Adam Kuper has succinctly summarized the difference between the two in noting that Tylor's definition amounted to no more than 'a list of traits, with the consequence that culture might be inventoried but never analysed' (Kuper 2000, p. 57). Boas also noted the difference. 'Even Tylor,' he once said, 'thought that scraps of data from here, there, and everywhere were enough for ethnology' (Boas cit. Benedict 1943, p. 3).

A number of issues coalesce here. The first concerns the transition from the style of armchair anthropology practiced by Tylor and the evolutionary assumptions underlying the typological method of museum displays which informed his collecting practices. Objects culled from diverse locations – by missionaries, traders, policemen or looters – were brought together in evolutionary sequences in testimony to a universal path of human development (Bennett 2004). Although Boas cut his anthropological teeth in projects directed by Tylor, the problem space that he went on to develop was, George Stocking (1968) contends, a quite different one in which the interpretation of fieldwork evidence made the specific patterns produced by the intermixing of the traits comprising any specific culture a particular historical problem that was not susceptible to any general laws of an evolutionary kind. Susan Hegeman develops this line of argument further seeing the Boasian fieldwork problematic as a key moment in the development of a new form of anthropological authority based on the anthropologist's unique ability to decipher the distinguishing qualities of other cultures. In place of a commitment to the collection of objects that could be put on display for all to see as evidence of a universal narrative of humanity, the Boasian paradigm substituted the more abstract object of 'cultures' which required special methods of collection alert to the interrelations between objects, myths, rituals, language, etc., within a specific way of life accessible only to the trained anthropologist immersed in the culture in question (Hegeman 1999). Each culture, as Boas put it, 'can be understood only as an historical growth determined by the social and geographical environment in which each people is placed and by the way in which it develops the cultural material that comes into its possession from the outside or through its own creativeness' (Boas 2010, p. 4).

It is in the manner in which this creative capacity is conceived that aesthetic conceptions entered into the organization of this new form of anthropological expertise. This is, however, a matter that was subject to different formulations at different moments in the development of the culture concept. Boas was notably reticent on the subject, implicitly drawing on the Germanic tradition to impute the creativity of a people to their unique genius, a capacity which he sometime interpreted in terms of Herder's categories, sometimes in terms of those provided by Humboldt and sometimes in Kantian terms (Stocking 1968, Bunzl 1996). As subsequently developed by his various students, however, the distinctive shape of a culture was re-interpreted in modernist terms as the result of a form-giving activity modelled on the work of art which, whether performed by individual or collective social agents, broke through inherited patterns of thought and behaviour to crystallize new social tendencies. The key intervention here was Edward Sapir's (1924) paper 'Culture, genuine and spurious'. Richard Handler summarizes the definition of culture proposed in this as consisting in: (1) 'the idea that a culture is a patterning of values that gives significance to the lives of those who hold them', (2) 'that people's participation in the pattern is "instinctive" – in other words, unconscious', (3) that in the case of genuine culture 'the patterning of values is aesthetically harmonious', and (4) that this harmony is expressive of 'a richly varied and yet somehow unified and consistent attitude toward life' (Handler 2005, p. 68).

It was this conception of a configurational order arising out of the form-giving principles that expressed the inner necessities of group life – of culture as 'an integrated spiritual totality which somehow conditioned the form of its elements' (Stocking 1968, p. 21) – that differentiated the Boasian culture concept from Malinowski's functional conception of the social whole as an amalgamation of the pragmatic functions performed by different traits. As such it played two distinctive roles in the organization of new forms of anthropological authority. 'Released from the burden of representing a coherent "humanity" and possessing a specialised knowledge of cultural *diversity*, Boas and his students became experts in the manipulation of cultural estrangement for the purposes of social critique' (Hegeman 1999, 46). Their fieldwork amongst others – most notably the Native Americans of the western seaboard and the Plains Indians – provided the anthropologist with privileged access to principles of alterity which, echoing modernist conceptions of the work of art as a defamiliarizing device, could then be used to make the distinctive properties of American culture and society perceptible in new ways. Anthropology, as Robert Lynd put it, had a 'priceless advantage over the other social sciences' (Lynd 1967, p. 156) derived from 'tilling the overlooked field of primitive cultures in the backward corners of the world' (p. 157) to give it a monopoly on the 'indispensable raw material of the social sciences'. The primitive other constituted an experimental test tube in which, 'boiled free of all the accompaniments of a capitalist economy', he provided 'for all the rest of us exact data on the range of human tolerance for institutional ways different from our own' (p. 157) which could then be used in order 'better understand and control our own culture' (p. 158).

The second role was implicit in this first one: the claim to have found in culture an object of study that would establish anthropology's claims to the status of an autonomous science with a distinct object of its own. This struggle for scientific autonomy was waged on a number of fronts: against biology and psychology; sometimes in alliance with, and sometimes against, sociology.[11] Alfred Kroeber's (1917) conception of culture as the superorganic was crucial to the first of these struggles, disputing post-Darwinian accounts of mechanisms of hereditary accumulation in the name of culture as a level of realities over and above those grounded in or arising out of the sequencing of organic life. While

Sapir and others explored possible synergies between anthropology and psychoanalysis, behaviourist psychology was similarly disposed of. For Robert Lowie, the culture concept established that:

> in so far as knowledge, emotion, and will are neither the result of natural endowment shared with other members of the species nor rest on an individual organic basis, we have a thing *sui generis* that demands for its investigation a distinct science. (Lowie 1996, p. 17)

This meant, he continued, that it must be considered 'autonomous with reference to psychology' (p. 26).

These different aspects of the culture concept were economically brought together by Ruth Benedict when she wrote that 'culture is more than a collection of mere isolated bits of behaviour. It is the integrated sum total of learned behaviour traits which are manifest by the members of a society' (Benedict 1947, p. 1). As such, its dependency on educative methods of acquisition and transmission disqualified biologically based mechanisms for the inheritance of acquired characteristics: 'It is essential to the concept of culture that instincts, innate reflexes, and any other biologically inherited forms of behaviour be ruled out' (p. 1). The undue focus on the collection of material culture by the earlier generation of armchair anthropologists was similarly chastised as misplaced:

> Strictly speaking, material culture is not really culture at all. ... Behind every artefact are the patterns of culture that give form to the idea for the artefact and the techniques of shaping and using it. ... The use and meaning of any object depends almost wholly on non-material behaviour patterns, and the objects derive their true significance from such patterns. (p. 1)

The unity of a culture derived from the aesthetic form-like properties that give a distinctive shape to ways of life is, though, Benedict contends, always a fractured one. Why? Because most of the traits that comprise the building blocks of a culture come from sources that 'are diverse and unlike' (p. 1), thus constituting contradictory elements which either cancel each other out or are brought together in a new form of synthesis. It is in the processes through which such new syntheses are produced that the aesthetic and the spatial aspects of the culture concept are brought together.

Mutable spatializations of cultures in movement

Let me go back to Williams again. In opening his essay 'Culture is ordinary', it is the connections between place and way of life that Williams first looks to in order to convey a sense of culture's ordinariness. 'To grow up in that country', he says, 'was to see the shape of a culture, and its modes of change' (Williams 1989, p. 4). The country in question – the Border Country between England and Wales – is richly evoked by recounting a bus journey from Hereford to the Black Mountains. Orchards, meadows, hillside bracken, early iron works, Norman castles, steel mills, pitheads, the railway, scattered farms, town terraces – this is the regional scene that Williams starts with before populating it by describing his own working-class affiliations to it through his father and grandfather. But it is the sense of a wider spatially defined culture that comes first, and class second. The complex interplay between these regional and class coordinates also spills over into questions of Englishness as, with T.S. Eliot in his sights, he insists that it is working-class culture – and not the petty niceties of the English ruling class – that gives English culture, understood as a way of life, its distinctive coherence. Welsh culture too, of course; however, in this essay, it is Englishness that most concerns Williams in pinning his colours to the principles of 'a distinct working-class way of life … with its emphases of neighbourhood, mutual obligation, and common betterment as … the best basis for any future English society' (p. 8). Ways of life are thus defined spatially as well socially; they are regionally embedded; and the relations between them are nationally defining.

In highlighting the relations between place and way of life, Williams followed in the footsteps of T.S. Eliot who included among the three main conditions for culture 'the necessity that a culture should be analysable, geographically, into local cultures' (Eliot 1962, Kindle loc. 70). And he acknowledges his debt to anthropologists in this regard: 'By "culture", then, I mean first of all what the anthropologists mean: the way of life of a particular people living together in one place' (loc. 1687).[12] Although these connections between culture and place were, in the Boasian tradition, fluid and mutable, they have often been read as binding different ways of life, people and territories into essentialist relations to one another. There are a number of reasons for this. Some have to do with the interpretation of the culture concept in the context of American assimilationist policies in the late 1920s and 1930s in which the conception of America as a melting pot defined an emerging American national self-consciousness that was differentiated from European nationalisms (Gilkeson 2010, Mandler 2013). Others derive from the territorialization of the culture concept during the 1939–1945 war and the post-war period when it was revised to refer to a field of national differences that were to be made commensurable with one another through the new geopolitical-diplomatic order of the United Nations (Orta 2004, Price 2008).

Some of Boas's early work also echoed Herder's conception of culture as the expression of a geographically delimited people. Later, however, he rejected any sense that regional environments might be regarded as having a determining influence on cultures. 'It is sufficient', he wrote in 1932, 'to see the fundamental differences of culture that thrive one after the other in the same environment, to make us understand the limitations of environmental influence', adding, as a pointed contrast, that the 'aborigines of Australia live in the same environment in which the White invaders live' (Boas 1982a, p. 256). The key questions here bear on Boasian conceptions of the relations between processes of cultural diffusion and the organization of cultural areas. These questions have been revisited in a substantial body of recent work which argues that the Boasian construction of these relations anticipates contemporary accounts of the relations between trans-border cultural flows and migration in breaking with the modernist order of nation states. It was, Ira Bashkow argues, 'axiomatic to the Boasians that cultural boundaries were porous and permeable', citing Robert Lowie's contention that any given culture is 'a "planless hodgepodge", a "thing of shreds and patches"' as economically summarizing the view that any particular culture 'develops not according to a fixed law or design but out of a vast set of contingent external influences' (Bashkow 2004, p. 445). These are brought into historically contingent, impermanent and unstable fusions with one another in particularly territorially marked culture areas, only to be later disaggregated in the context of different relations of cross-cultural contact and population migrations. Brad Evans similarly interprets Boas's significance as consisting not in his pluralization of the culture concept – something that Herder had already done – but in his conception of the 'detachability' of the texts and objects that comprise the elements of a culture from any organic association with any particular spatial or historical culture so that they might serve as 'vehicles for the articulation and disarticulation of meaning across discontinuous geographies and temporalities' (Evans 2005, p. 15). Recounting Boas's role in the reconceptualization of folklore studies under the influence of turn-of-the-century developments in philology, Evans argues that these undermined earlier romantic and nationalist conceptions of an inherent connection between a particular people and a particular culture by reconceptualizing cultures as being, like languages, 'public objects' formed by processes of historical interaction and migration beyond the control of individual speakers or speech communities.

The pattern of a culture, then, is not expressive of an essential set of relations between a people, place and way life but is a conjunctural and pliable articulation of those relations that derives its distinctive qualities from the creative, form-giving capacity of the people concerned. In turning now to consider how these spatial and aesthetic aspects of the culture concept informed the governmental rationalities that characterized the development of the relations between earlier 'settlers' and more recent immigrants, and between both of these and Native Americans and African-Americans, I engage with recent re-evaluations of the relations between the culture concept and racial categories.

The culture concept, race and assimilation

While the reappraisals of the Boasian tradition that I have drawn on above accentuate those aspects of the culture concept that resonate with contemporary accounts of processes of cultural hybridization, they are also careful to stress the differences. Moreover, many of the other qualities conventionally attributed to the culture concept – its rebuttal of hierarchical orderings of the relations between different cultures; its democratization of culture; and its critique of racial categories – do not withstand scrutiny. Although Boas contested the conception of 'primitive cultures' as having had no history ['even a primitive people has a long history behind it' (Boas 1974, p. 68)] the distinction between primitive and civilized peoples was never entirely jettisoned. It informs Boas's account of the difference between 'modern aesthetic feeling' (Boas 2010, p. 356) and that of the primitive and, more forthrightly, it shapes Clark Wissler's characterization of primitives as 'slackers in culture' who, while they 'have not stood still in so far as the content of their culture goes' are 'in the manner of rationalisation … on the chronological level of past ages' (Wissler 1923, pp. 326–327).[13]

The democratic register of the concept was also limited. To be sure, it was more democratic in class terms than its adaptation by Eliot. Contrast Robert Lowie's list of the elements of American culture with Eliot's subordination of the English way of life to a repertoire of ruling-class practices:

> The fact that your boy plays "button, button, who has the button?" is just as much an element of our culture as the fact that a room is lighted by electricity. So is the baseball enthusiasm of our grown-up populations, so are moving picture shows, *thésdansants*, Thanksgiving Day masquerades, bar-rooms, Ziegfeld Midnight Follies, evening schools, the Hearst papers, woman suffrage clubs, the single-tax movement, Riker drug stores, touring-sedans, and Tammany Hall. (Lowie 1966, pp. 6–7)

But what is missing here is any reference to the cultural practices of African-Americans, the new post-1890s cohorts of immigrants from southern Europe, or Native Americans. These exclusions were constitutive of the culture concept during this period. When Boas wrote about the 'creative genius' of Africans, it was always only with reference to traditional African culture in Africa. He took no account of the consequences of the Middle Passage or the contemporary cultural creativity of African-Americans even though he produced his most important work at the University of Columbia at the time of the Harlem Renaissance (Lamothe 2008, Zumwait 2008). And while, courtesy of the anthropological fieldworker, the cultures of Native Americans provide a defamiliarizing device that highlighted the distinctive qualities of American culture, there was never any sense – in Boas, in Benedict, or in Mead – that they might be counted a part of that culture. As Steven Conn (2004) has shown, Boasian anthropology played a key role in detaching Native Americans from the realms of American history and painting and assigning them to a timeless anthropological present that was in America, but not of it.

This bears on the third limitation of the culture concept: its relations to a set of biological race categories which excluded African-Americans and Native Americans from the machineries of assimilation that the concept established. This is not to discount the significance of Boas's persistent probing of racial accounts of human difference. 'It has not been possible', he wrote in 1920, 'to discover in the races of man any kind of fundamental biological differences that would outweigh the influence of culture' (Boas 1920, p. 35). This was, however, never a matter that he entirely put to rest. Throughout his career, and paralleling his 'fieldwork' among the Kwakiutal, the public school provided Boas with another context for collecting – not, though, stories, myths or languages, but anthropometric data relating to changes in the body types of second, relative to first, generation immigrants (Baker 2010, pp. 137–146). Boas conceived this work as a critical engagement with the problem space of anthropometry: 'we have to consider the investigation of the instability of the body under varying environmental conditions as one of the most fundamental subjects to be considered in an anthropometric study of our population' (Boas 1982b, p. 59). However, while demonstrating the plasticity of bodily types in ways that suggested that immigrants might be just as malleable in their physiognomies as in their ways of life, Boas – and his followers – retained a distinction between 'Caucasoid', 'Mongoloid' and 'Negroid' as biologically differentiated stocks of humanity. Although not organizing the relations between these in hierarchical terms, these categorizations led Boas to place the Negro in a different position from the immigrant with regard to processes of assimilation. He interpreted this as not just a cultural process but as a physio-anatomical one that would likely depend on the disappearance of the Negro as a distinct physical type through miscegenation. Arguing that this would lead to a progressive whitening of the black population, he concluded that the continued persistence of 'the pure negro type is practically impossible' (Boas 1974, p. 330).[14] The situation with regard to Native Americans was different but scarcely more auspicious. On the one hand, in racial terms, they hardly mattered. The degree of intermarriage between Indians and settlers, Boas argued, had not been sufficient in 'any populous part of the United States to be considered as an important element in our population' (Boas 1974, p. 319). Nicely distanced from the urban centres of metropolitan America, Native Americans were not a part of the mix from which the future of America's population stock or its culture was to be forged. The 'skeleton in the closet' of Boasian anthropology, William Willis has argued, consists in the fact that, when applied across the colour line separating Caucasian from other populations, its lessons regarding the plasticity and conjunctural mutability of inherited cultures was translated into the enculturation of coloured people into white culture.

'The transmission of culture from coloured peoples to white people was largely ignored', he argued, 'especially when studying North American Indians' (Willis 1999, p. 139). Either that or, in Ruth Benedict's conception, the cultures of the Indian and of white Americans had – after an initial period of interaction – come to face each other as two impermeable wholes, each unable to find any space for the values of the other within its own. 'The Indians of the United States', as she put it, 'have most of them become simply men without a cultural country. They are unable to locate anything in the white man's way of life which is sufficiently congenial to their old culture' (Benedict 1947, p. 1) and were thus located outside the melting point of an emerging American culture.

My account here draws on the work of Mark Anderson (2014), Kamala Visweswaran (2010) and, more particularly, Matthew Jacobson (1998) who interprets the significance of the culture concept in terms of the role it played, alongside changing conceptions of whiteness, in adjudicating capacities for citizenship against the backdrop of the longer history of American republic-anism. Jacobson focuses particularly on the 1924 Johnson-Reed Act as prompting a pivotal revision of the category of whiteness. Whereas whiteness and citizenship were linked in a 1790 Act of Congress according to a 'nativist' concept limiting citizenship to free white persons with rights of residence, the period from 1840 to 1924 witnessed a strategic redefinition of whiteness designed to address the dilemmas of American white nativism faced with new waves of immigration from diverse sources. This produced new racialized divisions within the earlier undifferentiated category of whiteness, disbarring some 'white' groups from the liberal criteria defining fitness for self-government by producing new shades of darkness that differentiated groups like the Poles and the Irish from Anglo-Saxons, the privileged representatives of white nativism.[15] The 1924 Act constituted a new articulation of this tendency in differentiating desirable European migrants (defined as 'Nordic', a wider category than Anglo-Saxon in that it also included German and Scandinavian migrants) from 'Alpines' and 'Mediterraneans' (who had been the main sources of new immigrants since the 1880s, and whose numbers were curtailed by this measure). The logic governing the revision of the category of whiteness after 1924, when the tensions around immigration from southern Europe lessened somewhat as a consequence of the reduction in their numbers, was, Jacobson argues one in which:

> the civic story of assimilation (the process by which the Irish, Russian Jews, Poles, and Greeks became Americans) is inseparable from the cultural story of racial alchemy (the process by which Celts, Hebrews, Slavs, and Mediterraneans became Caucasians. (Jacobson 1998, p. 8)

It was this conception of a project of assimilation organized around a newly homogenized category of the Caucasian defined against the categories of the Mongolian and the Negro that provided the political rationality informing the governmental mobilization of the culture concept. I have argued elsewhere the need to attend to the relations between the processes of 'making culture' and 'changing society', arguing that the cultural disciplines have played a key role in organizing distinctive 'working surfaces on the social' through which governmental practices are brought to bear on the conduct of conduct (Bennett 2013). The trajectory of the Boasian culture concept is a case in point. From the late 1920s through the 1930s and into the 1940s, the relations between the aesthetic conception of the pattern of culture, its spatial coordinates and its malleability came to inform a programme in which cultural planners, guided by anthropologists, were to regulate the conditions in which American society would creatively transform itself by absorbing immigrant cultures in an assimilationist logic which focused exclusively on the relations between different periods of European migration. The culture concept was, Anderson argues, integral to 'the larger processes whereby stigmatized European immigrant populations were "whitened" and rendered assimilable into the "American" mainstream' (Anderson 2014, p. 5). The key reference point for this governmental rationality was that of the 'third generation'. In applying the culture concept to ask what were the uniquely defining characteristics of the American character, Mead argued that Americans established their ties with one another by finding common points on the road that they were all expected to travel 'after their forebears came from Europe one or two or three generations ago' (Mead 1942, p. 28). It was a road defined by the forging of new ties and by a dialectic of 'remembrance and purposeful forgetting of European ancestry'; and an initial clinging to European ways of life in Little Italies followed by a scattering 'to the suburbs and the small towns, to an "American" way of life' (p. 29). It was in this sense, she argued, that 'however many generations we may actually boast of in this country, however real our lack of ties in the old world may be, we are all third generation' (p. 31). Negroes, Native Americans and, in some formulations, Jews were special cases to be dealt with differently.

Anthropology, Willis argued, was the discipline which, in one way or another, made non-white people into different human beings from white people. Whereas this had earlier been done by explicit racist ideologies, the Boasians achieved the same end through the concepts of culture and cultural relativism – sleights of hand, he suggests, which avoided black outrage at white dominance while retaining the status of non-whites as objects to be manipulated in a 'laboratory' setting, be it that of the field, the Indian reserve, or the public school. These were, however, more than just sleights of hand. They constituted, albeit partially and problematically, a displacement of not only race but also, as John Dewey recognized,[16] the primacy hitherto accorded individuals in liberal forms of rule as cultures, and the relations between them, were conceived as providing the working surfaces on the social – or, in Foucault's terms, the 'transactional realities' (Foucault 2008, p. 297) – through which the relations between the populations constituting a multicultural polity were to be managed. This was, however, a polity with its own constitutive exclusions.

Genealogical work on the archive

We can see, then, how the culture concept came to be aligned – in Turner's terms – with a project of 'making culture national' which American anthropology largely turned its back on during the critical fermentations of the 1960s. We can also understand the attractions of British cultural studies when, in the 1980s, its introduction to the American intellectual scene provided a critical alternative to this tradition.[17] If this owed a good deal to the influence of Williams's concept of culture as a way of life which, as we have seen, was defined primarily in terms of spatial and class coordinates, it owed more, over the longer term, to the work of Stuart Hall. For it was Hall who constituted the defining figure of cultural studies at its most critical point of entry into the USA and whose radical rethinking of the relations between race and ethnicity provided a productive alternative to the formulations of identity politics.[18]

The entry of cultural studies into Australia differed in a number of ways. It took place earlier; it was significantly mediated through literary studies; and it was, initially, more responsive to the distinctive articulation of the relations between class, aesthetics and the concept of culture as a way of life that characterized Williams's project of a common culture. This is not, though, the perspective from which, in his key text of the 1990s, Turner engages with the making and remaking of Australian culture. It is rather Hall he looks to in order to understand hybridity as a process of cultural fusion of diverse elements into distinctive and mobile configurations that disrupt and contest the logic of assimilation while also providing an account of how identities are made and remade on the part of mobile forces that avoids 'the trendy voyaging of the postmodern or simplistic versions of global homogenisation' (Hall cit Turner 1994, p. 124). Turner does, so moreover, without defining national cultures as singular, bound in an essentialist way to a particular territory. It is rather a set of cultures in contentious dialogues and negotiations with one another that has to be reckoned with in the expectation that these will generate inherent contradictions which reflect Australia's 'dual history as colonized and coloniser' (p. 123) and as an immigrant country and in which immigrant cultures serve as a source of its future cultural dynamism.

If these represent the positive directions in which Turner urges that Australian culture should be remade, he is equally well aware of the forces arrayed against it. Some of these were identified by Ghassan Hage's account of the changing governmental articulations of the field of whiteness during successive phases in the post-1970s development of Australian multicultural policies, practices and discourses (Hage 1998). There are strong parallels between this account and the governmental rationale that characterized the post-1924 deployment of the culture concept in America. They are, indeed, stronger than Hage recognizes. For Hage's focus on whiteness is restricted to its operation on and in the relations between different waves of Australia's migrant populations and their different degrees of whiteness. It accordingly pays little if any attention to the process through which Aborigines have been placed outside these frameworks. These issues come into sharper relief today when the political logics of Australia's multicultural programmes have become increasingly assimilationist while, at the same time, its immigration and Indigenous policies have introduced new forms of sequestration along racial lines with regard to refugees (through its border protection policies) while perpetuating long-standing forms of racial sequestration with regard to Indigenous Australians (through the Northern Territory Intervention and its successor programmes; see Macoun 2011). A part of my concern, then, has been to suggest that the longer history of the culture concept in its Boasian and post-Boasian American formations affords a means of effecting a closer dialogue between the intellectual and governmental deployments of the concept of culture in Australia and America in terms of their shared properties as settler colonial societies with similar histories of immigration.

There is, however, a further value to be derived from a more critical and extended engagement with the conceptual prehistories of cultural studies. The concepts of culture with which we work always come to us wagging their histories behind them. But sometimes those histories are too foreshortened and partial. Hall recognized this when urging the need for 'genealogical and archaeological work on the archive' to counter the tendency to assume that cultural studies emerged 'somewhere at that moment when I first met Raymond Williams or in the glance I exchanged with Richard Hoggart' (Hall 1992, p. 277). I have therefore sought to draw a longer bow and to shift the angle of vision by looking at the history of the culture concept within American anthropology. I have, however, done no more than scratch the surface of a history that has had a long reach. It was a history in which culture was first conceived as an object of knowledge that was detached from those of psychology, biology and the environmental disciplines and affiliated to the emerging objects of sociological knowledge; it was a history in which earlier aesthetic conceptions of culture were refashioned to provide a new stratum of intellectuals with a means of acting on the social by guiding the relations between different ways of life; and it was a history in which this capacity came to be connected to the distinctive values of America's liberal and democratic ways of life to the extent that such adjustments of the relations between cultures were to arise out of the activities of their members rather than from coercive state edicts (Dewey 1939).

It was also a history that helped to shape the roles that the culture as a way of life played in the early development of both British and Australian cultural studies.[19] Richard Handler, to recall an earlier aspect of my discussion, has commented on how Sapir's and Benedict's modernist concept of form helped to shape Williams' conception of the ordinariness of culture as something that is reshaped by the dynamic between the inherited repertoires of tradition and the creativity of a people. Handler also suggests that it is the notion of unconscious form that informs Richard Hoggart's account of working-class resistance to commercial mass culture. The 'pattern of working-class culture', he argues, 'is alive – adaptive, resistant, persistent – precisely because its "bearers", the "natives", hold to it unconsciously' (Handler 2005, pp. 163–164) albeit that this also accounts for, in Hoggart's estimation, its chief limitation: its inability to attain the forms of critical self-consciousness that are the hallmark of modernist literature. If this is one route, the literary route, through which the culture concept shaped the early formations of British cultural studies, its career, alongside a much wider set of initiatives that moved back and forth across the Atlantic during the 1939–1945 war and its immediate aftermath,[20] in pressing a case for culture as the most effective medium for the management of morale and the transformation of everyday habits, is another such route. We need to know more about both of these routes and, more crucially, their interactions to get a better sense of how cultural studies was initially shaped by projects aimed at the governance of conduct and the development of counter-conducts.

Acknowledgement

The research for this paper was conducted as a part of the research project Museum, Field, Metropolis, Colony: Practices of Social Governance' (DP110103776) funded by the Australian Research Council (ARC). I am grateful to the ARC for its support.

Disclosure statement

No potential conflict of interest was reported by the author.

Notes

1   Evans (2005, p. 5) offers an especially pertinent discussion of the limitations of Williams' discussion with regard to the American development of the culture concept over the closing decades of the nineteenth century and the opening decade of the twentieth century.
2   See, for example, Darnel (1998). The good reasons I refer to concern the role the concept played in shaping a distinctive American sense of culture. However, having made the point, I shall henceforth use the more user-friendly 'American' in referring to this tradition.

3   The only source I have come across that affiliates its concerns specifically to those of cultural studies is Molloy (2008), but this is to a rather loose sense of cultural studies as an interdisciplinary project. A search of the *Cultural Studies* website for 'Boas' turned up only five references, two of which were to earlier papers of mine, where the Boasian tradition is addressed only incidentally. Searches of *Continuum*, the *International Journal of Cultural Studies* and *Communication and Critical Cultural Studies* turned up similar results.

4   In her correspondence with her publisher, Benedict notes that 'Integrations of Culture' or 'Configurations of Culture' were her preferred titles from the point of view of exactness, but she felt they were too 'clumsy and Latinized' compared to 'Patterns' – 'a pleasant English word'. Ruth Fulton Benedict Papers, Vassar College Libraries, Archives and Special Collections, Series XVI, Margaret Mead, Folder 120.27 Patterns of Culture. See also Modell (2004).

5   Hubble (2006) engages with Mass Observation as a prelude to aspects of cultural studies; Mandler (2013) provides a detailed account of the role of anthropology in American and British approaches to the conception and management of morale in the 1939–1945 War; Groth and Lusty (2013, pp. 158–159) show the influence of the concept of 'culture patterns' on Mass Observation approaches to the analysis of dreams.

6   The final chapter of Gilkeson (2010) offers a detailed discussion of the reactions of American anthropologists to the importation of cultural studies.

7   See, for example, Brown (2003), Hegeman (1999) and Manganaro (2002).

8   I place 'postcolonial' in quotes since – as Turner recognizes – Australia remains a settler colony so far it relations to Indigenous Australians are concerned.

9   Larry Grossberg has taken issue with this aspect of Turner's work, arguing that such processes of theoretical hybridization are a generally shared characteristic of the conjunctural, context specificity that he imputes to cultural studies as a practice. He has also lodged a wider objection to any attempt to articulate cultural studies to geography by seeking to define nationally specific traditions urging, instead, the need to 'displace' cultural studies. [I refer to the essay 'Where is the "America" in American cultural studies?' in Grossberg (1997)].

10   And, of course, Turner's own account of British cultural studies (Turner 1996) played a key role here.

11   There was a good deal of overlap between the anthropological concept of culture and the concept of society developed by Parsonian sociology. See Kroeber and Parsons (1958) for an attempt to legislate an agreed division of conceptual territory between the two disciplines.

12   See Manganaro (2002) for a detailed discussion of the influence of American anthropology on Eliot.

13   While there are partial overlaps between Boas's and Wissler's work on culture areas, Wissler affiliated to the eugenic camp in opposition to Boas's

position on the racial questions that divided early twentieth century anthropology. See Spiro (2002).

14   Boas position here echoed the formulations of John Wesley Powell, the head of the Bureau of American Ethnology, and the key figure in late-nineteenth-century American anthropology. However, it has a longer history. It was a commonly held belief of slave owners in the mid-nineteenth century; Frederick Douglas (2000, p. 55) refers to it in his famous narrative of slave life. These aspects of the Boasian tradition help to explain why, although they had some personal and political connections, W.E.B. Du Bois never embraced Boas's culture concept (Evans 2005)

15   While there is not space to go fully into the matter, Julien Carter (2007) builds on Jacobson's discussion to illuminate the sexual dynamics that accompanied these developments as new norms of heterosexuality reinforced racialized divisions between Caucasian and other groups through the unequal distribution of the capacity for governing the passions that they attested to.

16   Dewey's *Freedom and Culture* (Dewey 1939) offers an eloquent discussion of the significance of the anthropological concept of culture in offering the potential to entirely transform the problematics of liberal government in these regards. I have discussed this elsewhere (Bennett 2014).

17   See especially on this the final chapter of Gilkeson (2010). Handler (2004) also alludes to the perturbations occasioned among anthropologists by this intrusion of an interloper into what they had regarded as their key conceptual terrain at precisely the moment they were abandoning it.

18   Grossberg (1997) refers particularly to the work of Hall and Paul Gilroy in this regard.

19   The Boasian culture concept also impacted on post-war French anthropology in varied ways. It contributed to Claude Levi-Strauss's conversion to pluralist and relativist understanding of cultures (Descola 2013, p. 75) and to the development of Pierre Bourdieu's concept of cultural capital. Bourdieu's familiarity with the work of Melville Herskovits, a Boas protégé, provided a model of distinctly cultural mechanisms of inheritance as an alternative to biological ones (Robbins 2005, pp. 16–20).

20   See, for an account of such projects more closely related to the social sciences, Rose (1999).

References

Anderson, M. (2014) 'Ruth Benedict, Boasian anthropology and the problem of the colour line', *History and Anthropology*, vol. 25, no. 3, pp. 395–414.

Baker, L. D. (2010) *Anthropology and the Racial Politics of Culture*, Durham, NC, and London, Duke University Press.

Bashkow, I. (2004) 'A Neo-Boasian conception of cultural boundaries', *American Anthropologist*, vol. 106, no. 3, pp. 443–458.

Benedict, R. (1943) 'Boas's contributions to ethnology', unpublished paper, Ruth Fulton Benedict Papers, Folder 49.5.

Benedict, R. (1947) 'The growth of culture', unpublished paper, Ruth Fulton Benedict Papers, Folder 54.7.

Bennett, T. (1998) *Culture: A Reformer's Science*, Sydney, Allen and Unwin; London, Sage.

Bennett, T. (2004) *Pasts Beyond Memory: Evolution, Museums, Colonialism*, London and New York, Routledge.

Bennett, T. (2013) *Making Culture, Changing Society*, London and New York, Routledge.

Bennett, T. (2014) 'Liberal government and the practical history of anthropology', *History and Anthropology*, vol. 25, no. 2, pp. 150–170.

Boas, F. (1974) 'Race problems in America', in *A Franz Boas Reader: The Shaping of American Anthropology, 1893–1911*, ed. G. W. Stocking, Chicago, IL, and London, University of Chicago Press, pp. 318–330. (Originally published 1909).

Boas, F. (1920) *Race and Democratic Society*, New York, J.J. Augustin.

Boas, F. (1982a) 'The aims of anthropological research', in *Race, Language and Culture*, ed. F. Boas, Chicago and London, University of Chicago Press, pp. 243–259. (Originally published 1932).

Boas, F. (1982b) 'Report on an anthropometric investigation of the population of the United States', in Boas (Originally published 1922).

Boas, F. (2010) *Primitive Art*, New York, Dover Publications. (Originally published 1927).

Brown, B. (2003) *A Sense of Things: The Object Matter of American Literature*, Chicago, University of Chicago Press.

Bunzl, M. (1996) 'Franz Boas and the Humboldtian Tradition: from Volksgeist and Nationalcharakter to an anthropological concept of culture', in *Volksgeist as Method and Ethic: Essays on Boasian Anthropology and the German Anthropological*

Tradition, ed. G. Stocking Jr, Madison, WI, University of Wisconsin Press, pp. 17–78.

Carter, J. B. (2007) *The Heart of Whiteness: Normal Sexuality and Race in America, 1880–1940,* Durham and London, Duke University Press.

CCCS. (2013) 'Fifth report 1968–69 (published October 1959). Part I: The centre – establishment, field of Study, etc', *Cultural Studies*, vol. 27, no. 5, pp. 880–886.

Conn, S. (2004) *History's Shadow: Native Americans and Historical Consciousness in the Nineteenth Century*, Chicago and London, University of Chicago Press.

Darnel, R. (1998) *And Along Came Boas. Continuity and Revolution in Americanist Anthropology*, Amsterdam/Philadelphia, John Benjamins Publishing Company.

Descola, P. (2013) *Beyond Nature and Culture*, Chicago and London, University of Chicago Press.

Dewey, J. (1939) *Freedom and Culture*, New York, G.P. Putnam's Sons.

Dollard, J. (1957) *Caste and Class in a Southern Town*, New York, Doubleday Anchor.

Douglas, F. (2000) *Narrative of the Life of Frederick Douglas, an American Slave*, New York, The Modern Library.

Eagleton, T. (2000) *The Idea of Culture*, Oxford, Blackwell.

Eliot, T. S. (1962) *Notes towards the Definition of Culture*, London, Faber and Faber.

Evans, B. (2005) *Before Culture: The Ethnographic Imagination in American Literature, 1865–1920*, Chicago, University of Chicago Press.

Fiske, J., Hodge, B. & Turner, G. (1987) *Myths of Oz: Reading Australian Popular Culture*, Sydney, Allen and Unwin.

Foucault, M. (2008) *The Birth of Biopolitics: Lectures at the Collège de France, 1978–1979*, London, Palgrave Macmillan.

Gilkeson, J. (2010) *Anthropologists and the Discovery of America*, Cambridge, Cambridge University Press.

Grossberg, L. (1997) *Bringing It All Back Home: Essays on Cultural Studies*, Durham, NC, and London, Duke University Press.

Groth, H. & Lusty, N. (2013) *Dreams and Modernity*, London and New York, Routledge.

Hage, G. (1998) *White Nation: Fantasies of White Supremacy in a Multicultural Society*, Sydney: Pluto Press.

Hall, S. (1992) 'Cultural studies and its theoretical legacies', in *Cultural Studies*, ed. L. Grossberg, C. Nelson & P. Treichler, New York and London, Routledge, pp. 277–294.

Hall, S. & Jefferson, T., eds. (1975) *Resistance through Rituals: Youth Subcultures in Post-War Britain*, London, Hutchinson/CCCS.

Handler, R. (2004) 'Afterword: mysteries of culture', *American Anthropologist*, vol. 106, no. 3, pp. 488–494.

Handler, R. (2005) *Critics against Culture: Anthropological Observers of Mass Society*, Madison, WI, University of Wisconsin Press.

Hegeman, S. (1999) *Patterns for America: Modernism and the Concept of Culture*, Princeton, NJ, Princeton University Press.

Hubble, N. (2006) *Mass Observation and Everyday Life: Culture, History, Theory*, London, Palgrave Macmillan.

Hunter, I. (1988) 'Settling limits to culture', *New Formations*, vol. 4, pp. 103–124.

Jacobson, M. F. (1998) *Whiteness of a Different Color: European Immigrants and the Alchemy of Race*, Cambridge, MA, Harvard University Press.

Kroeber, A. L. (1917) 'The superorganic', *American Anthropologist*, vol. 19, no. 2, pp. 163–213.

Kroeber, A. L. & Kluckhohn, C. (1952) *Culture: A Critical Review of Concepts and Definitions*, Cambridge, MA, Papers of the Peabody Museum of American Archaeology and Ethnology, Harvard University.

Kroeber, A. L. & Parsons, T. (1958) 'The concepts of culture and of social system', *American Sociological Review*, vol. 23, no. 5, pp. 582–590.

Kuper, A. (2000) *Culture: The Anthropologists' Account*, Cambridge, MA, Harvard University Press.

Lamothe, D. (2008) *Inventing the New Negro: Narrative, Culture and Ethnography*, Philadelphia, PA, University of Pennsylvania Press.

Lowie, R. (1966) *Culture and Ethnology*, New York, Basic Books. (Originally published 1917).

Lynd, R. S. (1967) *Knowledge for What? The Place of Social Sciences in American Culture*, Princeton, NJ, Princeton University Press. (Originally published 1939).

Lynd, R. & Lynd, H. M. (1929) *Middletown: A Study in Modern American Culture*, San Diego, CA, New York, and London, Harcourt Crace & Co.

Macoun, A. (2011) 'Aboriginality and the northern territory intervention', *Australian Journal of Political Science*, vol. 46, no. 3, pp. 519–534.

Mandler, P. (2013) *Return from the Natives: How Margaret Mead won the Second World War and Lost the Cold War*, New Haven, CT, and London, Yale University Press.

Manganaro, M. (2002) *Culture, 1922: The Emergence of a Concept*, Princeton, NJ, Princeton University Press.

Mead, M. (1942) *And Keep Your Powder Dry: An Anthropologist Looks at America*, New York, William Morrow and Company.

Modell, J. (2004) '"It is besides a pleasant English word" – Ruth Benedict's concept of patterns revisited', in *Reading Benedict / Reading Mead: Feminism, Race, and Imperial Visions*, ed. Dolores Janiewski & Lois W. Banner, Baltimore, MD, and London, Johns Hopkins University Press, pp. 203–228.

Molloy, M. (2008) *On Creating a Usable Culture: Margaret Mead and the Emergence of American Cosmopolitanism*, Honolulu, HI, University of Hawai'i Press.

Orta, A. (2004) 'The promise of particularism and the theology of culture: limits and lessons of "neo-Boasianism"', *American Anthropologist*, vol. 106, no. 3, pp. 473–487.

Price, D. H. (2008) *Anthropological Intelligence: The Deployment and Neglect of American Anthropology in the Second World War*, Durham, NC, and London, Duke University Press.

Robbins, D. (2005) 'The origins, early development and status of Bourdieu's concept of "cultural capital"', *British Journal of Sociology*, vol. 56, no. 1, pp. 13–30.

Rose, N. (1999) *Governing the Soul: The Shaping of the Private Self*, London, Free Association Books.

Sapir, E. (1924) 'Culture, genuine and spurious', *American Journal of Sociology*, vol. 29, pp. 401–429.

Spiro, J. P. (2002) 'Nordic vs. anti-Nordic: the Galton Society and the American Anthropological Association', *Patterns of Prejudice*, vol. 36, no. 1, pp. 35–48.

Stocking, G. W. Jr (1968) 'Franz Boas and the culture concept in historical perspective', in *Race, Culture, and Evolution: Essays in the History of Anthropology*, ed. G. W. Stocking, Jr, New York, Free Press, pp. 195–233.

Turner, G. (1986) *National Fictions: Literature, Film and the Construction of Australian Narrative*, Sydney, Allen and Unwin.

Turner, G. (1994) *Making it National: Nationalism and Popular Culture*, Sydney, Allen and Unwin.

Turner, G., ed. (1993) *Nation, Culture, Text: Australian Cultural and Media Studies*, London and New York, Routledge.

Turner, G. (1996) *British Cultural Studies: An Introduction*, London and New York, Routledge.

Turner, G. & Pertierra, A. C. (2013) *Locating Television: Zones of Consumption*, London and New York, Routledge.

Tylor, E. B. (1871) *Primitive Culture: Researches into the Development of Mythology, Philosophy, Religion, Language, Art and Custom*, London, J. Murray.

Visweswaran, K. (2010) *Un/common Cultures: Racism and the Rearticulation of Cultural Difference*, Durham, NC, and London, Duke University Press.

Whyte, W. H. (1993) *Street Corner Society: The Social Structure of an Italian Slum*, Chicago, IL, University of Chicago Press.

Williams, R. (1965) *The Long Revolution*, Harmondsworth, Penguin.

Williams, R. (1989) 'Culture is ordinary', in *Resources of Hope: Culture, Democracy, Socialism*, ed. R. Williams, London, Verso, pp. 3–14. (Originally published 1958).

Williams, R. (1976) *Keywords: A Vocabulary of Culture and Society*, London, Fontana/Croom Helm.

Willis, W. S. Jr (1999) 'Skeletons In the anthropological closet', in *Reinventing Anthropology*, ed. D. Hymes, Ann Arbor, MI, University of Michigan Press, pp. 121–151.

Wissler, C. (1923) *Man and Culture*, New York, Thomas Y. Crowell Company.

Wolfe, P. (1999) *Settler Colonialism and the Transformation of Anthropology: The Politics and Poetics of an Ethnographic Event*, London, Cassell.

Zumwait, R. L. (2008) *Franz Boas and W.E.B. Du Bois at Atlanta University, 1906*, Philadelphia, PA, American Philosophical Society.

John C. Byron

POLITICS AS SCHOLARLY PRACTICE

Graeme Turner and the art of advocacy

In addition to his very considerable and influential body of scholarship, and his roles as a pathfinder and senior leader of cultural studies in Australia and beyond, Graeme Turner has made a profound if less well-known contribution as an advocate and adviser at the national level, for cultural studies and the wider humanities. Turner's election in 2004 as President of the Australian Academy of the Humanities was greeted by elements of the conservative commentariat as the final proof of the complete annihilation of sense and meaning in Australian universities. Within four years, Turner had garnered sufficient respect to be appointed personally to the nation's preeminent science and research advisory body, the Prime Minister's Science, Engineering and Innovation Council, a distinction confirmed by his reappointment in 2012. This article offers an intimate account of Turner's advocacy and policy activities, detailing many of the achievements, along with some of the frustrating near-misses, of his work during and after his Presidency. It traces his development from a seasoned institutional player and accomplished scholar, encountering the dual challenges of slippery politics and leaden bureaucracy, to his rapid emergence as an expert political operator quite at home (if a little cold) in Canberra. The article proposes a theory of Turner's approach, beyond his well-known work ethic, intellectual acuity and force of personality, conceiving of his advocacy and policy work as a species of cultural studies itself – an enactment of a politically engaged cultural practice – as much as an initiative on its behalf. This account looks back to Turner's own cultural scholarship for insights into his deployment of a highly sophisticated intellectual toolkit in a theoretically informed practice, to gain the attention, respect and support of politicians, public servants, industry leaders and the powerful science lobby.

This issue is full of accounts of Graeme Turner's prodigious contribution to cultural studies, to Australian research and to so many scholars' careers. The sheer scale of his presence in the life of the humanities in Australia over four decades is extraordinary, and his reach extends well beyond our shores as well. Graeme's work simply matters, in ways that touch so many of us: his intelligence and capacity for hard work are matched only by his generosity and collegial spirit. His professional life has been very much a collaborative one, based around mentorship, cooperation and support.

Most of this activity has taken place in public, but many will not know of his work behind closed doors, in the corridors of Canberra. It is my view that Graeme's advocacy in the national policy arena is every bit as important, penetrating and enduring as his work as a scholar, author, teacher, mentor and disciplinary leader. I saw this work up close at the Australian Academy of the Humanities (AAH), where Graeme was President (November 2004 to November 2007), and I was Executive Director (August 2003 to May 2010). We became an effective team and great mates, and our close collaboration continued well after his term had finished.

This article is primarily concerned with the circumstances that imposed upon Graeme while he was President of the Academy, and the way he went about doing the job. It sketches that advocacy leadership role, and summarizes the prevailing attitudes towards the humanities in Australia at the time. It then outlines some of the challenges Graeme confronted during his term. The article then proposes a theory of his *modus operandi* in advocacy that is rooted in his cultural studies scholarship, and closes with a brief overview of his work since the end of his Presidency.

Several war stories are recounted below in broad terms, but there are no confidences betrayed here, nor trade secrets revealed. It is my conviction that trust is the currency of politics, and that effective policy-making and advocacy sometimes require confidentiality; otherwise, candour can only retreat, and the capacity to collaborate, experiment and convince will be seriously diminished.

Furthermore, I mean no harm to the principals of this story, many of whom are still working actively, either in their old lines of work – in politics, the universities, the media and advocacy organizations – or in new roles in public life. The accounts from this period have been more or less settled (for further information, see Presidents Reports 2003–2010, McCalman 2004, Haigh 2006, Turner 2006b, Carr 2013).

Accordingly, this narrative concerns itself primarily with the public events, and what they reveal about Graeme's approach. In doing so, I hope I am able to offer some sense of the extraordinary effort that Graeme expended on behalf of us all, and the intelligence and acumen he marshalled, to remarkable effect.

The Academy

Graeme Turner was elected President of the AAH one pleasant Hobart afternoon in November 2004. The election placed him at the helm of the body that comprises and represents the preeminent scholars and practitioners in the humanities in Australia (numbering 422 at the time of his election).

While the AAH is a discrete, independent entity, its functions largely resemble the humanities branches of foreign organizations such as the British Academy, the American Academy of Arts and Sciences and their counterparts around the world (although some of its activities more closely align in North America with the American Council of Learned Societies and the Canadian Federation of Humanities and Social Sciences). The Academy was created by Royal Charter in 1969 and is one of the four Australian Learned Academies (along with the Academies of Social Sciences, Science and Technological Sciences and Engineering).

According to the Academy's Royal Charter and By-Laws, the President's role is chiefly concerned with the diligent operation of the organization itself. In practice, this work is delegated to the Secretariat through the Executive Director, with oversight by the President and Council. The real job lies elsewhere.

Upon his election, Graeme effectively became the nation's unofficial Chief Humanist: the first port of call for advice, comment and policy input from politicians, the public service, the (official) Chief Scientist, the media and the university sector. It also put him at the interface between our Academy and related advocacy organizations, including the other Academies. These functions generated most of the heat and light during Graeme's Presidency. As his Executive Director, I worked closely with Graeme in these advocacy, policy advisory and diplomatic activities, and represented him in the capital between visits.

Leadership of the scholarly humanities in Australia involves a lot of listening and the preparedness to reformulate long-held perspectives, as much as it does the provision of guidance, advice and encouragement. It requires, by turns, diplomacy, frankness, fine judgement, courage, charisma, discretion and action: and the knack of knowing which stratagem. This aspect of the President's role both produces and is produced by the other three components of management, advocacy and collaboration. In reality, Graeme had been one of the country's senior discipline leaders in the humanities for some time before his election, in cultural studies and its cognates. His election only broadened the scope of this experienced leadership across the full range of humanities scholarship.

The operating environment

Disciplinary leadership is never an easy job, but there is good reason to suspect it is a somewhat harder in the humanities than it is the natural and physical sciences, say. As anyone reading *Cultural Studies* will be well aware, we are often the easiest dog to kick whenever a rant is due on academics, intellectuals, 'wasteful' research funding or the problem with kids these days (postmodernism, apparently – regarding which, more below). Australian culture has a hard, practical, no-nonsense edge, which occasionally comes together with its cultural insecurities and distrust of anything too bookish to produce an unpleasant anti-intellectualism with little tolerance for those it sees as effete, pretentious wankers concerned with the outré and peripheral. Australians are not alone in this tendency, of course, but the venom with which it is occasionally expressed here surprises even hardened northern hemisphere colleagues. Setting the hounds baying for arts faculty blood is a classic set piece move in the Australian populist playbook: it has become a markedly dog-eared page, even for that well-foxed volume.

Among the mockery and disdain aimed at the humanities generally, the paroxysms reserved for cultural studies seem to be particularly rabid. In this respect, the Australian experience perhaps cleaves nearer to that of other jurisdictions: we all have our scars. Cultural studies must be punished for mining advances in the humanities, arts, social sciences, natural sciences, the media, technology, industry and society at large, to fuel its hunger for theoretical innovation. It is precisely these strange, counter-intuitive, experimental theoretical approaches that are routinely and savagely attacked by the conservative media, by politicians and sometimes by other academics. Within this discourse of admonition, these perspectives are typically named 'postmodernism', regardless of the technical accuracy of the term. The use of this label in mainstream outlets such as newspapers, magazines and political speeches magically bestows upon the speaker an absolute and irrevocable licence for ridicule, even – perhaps especially – when it is exercised from a position of sublime ignorance.

Not every critique is unwarranted or unschooled; of course, some commentary comes from a position of sincere intellectual engagement, and it is fair to say that in some instances it is a fair cop. This more salient critique is usually scholarly in origin, and tends to savour of earnestness tinged with a little regret. However, the bulk of the attack on the humanities before and during the period in question contrasted starkly. In the mainstream media, the conservative outlets and the political discourse, it was characterized by a bully-boy savagery and was almost always constructed around straw man arguments. These attacks on 'postmodernism' often lacked even a passing familiarity with the ideas supposedly under critique. They were unsophisticated, anti-intellectual and theoretically weightless, propelled by ideological fervour and concerned only with the surface of things, precisely the charges they themselves were levelling at the humanities. The irony was as delicious as it was infuriating.

Cultural studies' interest in everyday life and mainstream culture is another basis for unrestrained attack. The quotidian is judged an unsuitable focus of advanced enquiry, although reasons are seldom advanced: daily life is deemed, *prima facie*, to be unimportant, its mechanisms and meanings utterly apparent. On the grounds of both triviality and simplicity, according to this view, it is

82

taken for granted that the world in which we move every day is neither worthy nor in need of examination.

On the positive side, these sorts of attacks in the media and in the political realm turn out to be readily susceptible to inquiry as discursive events in themselves, by means of the implements lying about in the cultural studies toolbox.

Australia, then, is not an easy place to be the *de facto* Chief Humanist. That is an eternal verity: in late 2004, for a cultural studies maven, it was a vast understatement. At the same time, as it turns out, few academicians could have been better equipped to respond to the challenges with intellectual rigour, theoretical sophistication and extensive practical experience than Graeme Turner.

Prelude to a tempest

The period leading up to Graeme's assumption of the Presidency had offered a curious blend of adversity and opportunity. On the one hand, the kind of abuse outlined above came in waves, from various quarters. The Academy found itself engaged in constant debate with a range of critics on the value of humanities research. Some skirmishes focused on specific researchers or projects, while others were concerned with whole fields or approaches. Inevitably, these debates extended beyond their immediate parameters to draw in related fields, sometimes the whole of the humanities.

Furthermore, all this took place within (and as a special case of) a wider context of constant attacks on universities, the education sector generally, the arts, the national public broadcaster, trade unions, the not-for-profit sector, and anything else that smelled suspiciously progressive or inclusive, whether or not it was of 'the Left'. And consent for this barrage came from the very top.

Prime Minister John Howard had been head of the conservative Coalition Government since 1996. He was steaming towards what would prove to be his fourth consecutive win, an emphatic mandate to govern for another three years with an increased majority. A follower rather than leader of public opinion, Howard was quite comfortable playing to the cheap seats with crude attacks on 'political correctness', 'cultural elites' and the perfidy of publicly funded intellectuals; indeed, the staff of all public institutions were fair game. In this project, the Prime Minister was ably assisted by the right-wing media, especially the tabloid newspaper columnists and the 'shock-jock' talkback radio hosts.

This politically led conservative antagonism placed the Academy in a tricky position. The vast majority of Australian humanities scholarship takes place within the (overwhelmingly public) university system; humanities research in Australia is funded almost exclusively through the Australian Research Council (ARC); and the Academy is itself reliant upon an annual Grant-in-Aid. The

Federal Government funds all of these wholly or significantly and with a high degree of discretion.

The challenge was to defend colleagues from attack while advancing the case for humanities inclusion in science-oriented programs; to object to assaults on crucial public institutions like the Australian Broadcasting Corporation and the National Library, while seeking support for schemes to advance the next generation of humanities scholars. Graeme's immediate predecessors, Iain McCalman and Malcolm Gillies, had walked that exceedingly fine line with great skill and brio: they were (and remain today) very active defenders and proponents of the humanities, mounting both rear-guard actions and charm offensives, as required.

On the positive side, recent years of organizational reform had transformed the Academy into a professional, policy-oriented outfit that commanded attention and respect in the capital. It had good standing within both the ARC and the Department of Education, Science and Training; some friends inside the Australian Parliament; a solid network of support around the nation's university leadership; and a productive working relationship with the sector media.

The views of our Minister, Dr Brendan Nelson, were also encouraging. In a Budget night press release of May 2003, he had said:

> The humanities, arts and social sciences are critically important to the future development of Australia. Not only do they play a key role in supporting the national innovation system, they make a significant contribution to the development of our society, culture and individual identity. It is from this sector especially that the soul is passed from one generation to the next. (Nelson 2003)

Moreover, these were not new or passing sentiments. While still a backbencher, Nelson had expressed the view that, even when all the big scientific problems were solved, all the important questions would remain unanswered, without the accompanying development of society, culture and the arts (Nelson 1999). Additionally, we had found Nelson to be quite accessible, considering his busy schedule, and the senior officials within his portfolio to be well disposed (often an expression of Ministerial outlook).

Regrettably, the Minister's refined scruples proved unequal to the klaxon panic that assailed his political instincts, once push inevitably met shove.

The moment that was to prove pivotal to Graeme's Presidency came a year and a day before his election, in an article entitled 'Grants to Grumble' in Melbourne's *Herald Sun* tabloid newspaper by Murdoch columnist Andrew Bolt (Bolt 2003). The occasion was the annual ARC major grants announcement. Bolt had been scooped by a Murdoch colleague in Queensland, the *Sunday Mail*'s David English, whose '$450,000 to Study Mobile Phone' attacked Gerard Goggin's research (English 2003). (This attack soon backfired when the industry co-funders defended the research, which would produce sorely needed and highly commercial insights into their customers' usage behaviour.) But it was Bolt's article that made the government sit up and take notice.

In his habitual testicular style, Bolt savaged the Government and the ARC for funding projects he considered wasteful of public money. He ridiculed a number of senior humanities academics and their projects, impugned the ARC and its processes and raised doubts about the seriousness of the responsible Minister (our man, Brendan Nelson). At first glance, the article looked like nothing more than an unusually abusive iteration of the annual bullocking of the humanities from the right-wing press. It turned out to be the opening salvo in a battle that was to rage for several years to come.

What happened next was this.[1] The Federal Treasurer, Peter Costello, marched purposefully into the following Cabinet meeting, *Herald Sun* in hand. Showing the paper to Nelson and slapping it with his other hand, he boomed, 'So THIS is how you spend my money'?

Costello's loud admonition, delivered with his trademark smirk, completely silenced all other conversation in the Cabinet Room. The Treasurer read out a few choice cuts from the column. For those not familiar with Bolt's style, his is a particularly gamey version of the fare served up by the tabloid organs of the global Murdoch media empire, and he had excelled himself with that article. When delivered by the imposing Costello, the effect was devastating. Everybody laughed, if a little nervously: Nelson was acutely embarrassed and blanched visibly. My witness claims not to have been alone in thinking the brash, conceited Costello had been a bully, nor in having felt a little sorry for the genial, measured Nelson. But the damage had been done. The following year, in 2004, Nelson did not miss the chance to make his bones.

Chief humanist – Academy Presidency, 2004–2007

The day before Graeme was elected President, on 19 November 2004, the Government released the annual ARC major grants announcement. Innocuous enough on its own, the release was keenly studied by the academicians gathered in Hobart for the Academy's annual symposium. Congratulations and commiserations were distributed, tinged with envy and *schadenfreude*. The subtle reordering of academic prestige immediately commenced.

But the sorting of the blessed and the neglected was followed almost immediately by rumours that something had gone wrong; that the peer review grant selection process had been subject to some inappropriate interference. Some of the senior scholars present clearly knew something was amiss, from their participation on the ARC's Expert Advisory Panel for Creative Arts and Humanities. They were bound by a Pythagorean vow of silence and were limited to muttering among themselves in dark corners, but the impression soon diffused that some projects recommended for funding had fallen off the list somewhere along the line.

Over the ensuing week, Graeme and I each made our different enquiries. The ever-professional ARC staff would make no comment, on or off the record, but a Government political staffer confided to me that there had apparently been Ministerial intervention. Not only that, but a Point Was Being Made.

Confirmation came a week later in the form of a triumphant column by our old mate Andrew Bolt. In 'Paid to be Pointless', published on 26 November 2004, Bolt praised Minister Nelson's decision to get tough with the humanities by vetoing three projects that had been recommended for funding (Bolt 2004). Bolt modestly claimed all the credit for this tough, new, no-nonsense regime, under which projects he deemed unworthy had been torpedoed. His onanistic urges temporarily gratified, Bolt then moved on to address the projects that had still made it through. He tempered his praise of the hair on the Minister's chest with the lament that it was not thicker: a more manly thatch, Bolt implied, might have inspired Nelson to veto some of these others, as well (especially any of a sexual nature, which is apparently a particular anxiety of Mr Bolt's).

To be clear, there was nothing legally improper about the Minister's actions: politically and procedurally improper, certainly, but not legally improper. Under the *Australian Research Council Act 2001*, ARC grants are awarded by the Minister alone (Commonwealth of Australia 2001), operating on the delegated authority of the Parliament. Beyond the appropriated budget available, the Minister needs no Cabinet guidance or approval for the decision. In the other direction, the ARC CEO and the College merely provide advice to inform the Ministerial decision. Although Nelson's action is widely referred to as a veto, technically he withheld his approval, in the face of expert advice to give it. Please do not mistake my meaning: in reality, a veto is exactly what it was; and in my view Nelson's actions were doubly reprehensible. In the first place, they constituted an exercise of political power in the clear awareness of relative ignorance. Nelson has his quirks, but in my experience he is not intellectually vain: unlike many of the right-wing pundits of the media and around the Cabinet table, he did not imagine that he had a better grasp of the advanced intellectual content than the academic experts on his advisory panels. To self-consciously ignore genuine expertise, then, savours of a wilful exercise in imperial fiat. It is somehow worse than acting under the risible delusion (apparently harboured by Bolt and his ilk) of actually knowing better than the experts. Furthermore, the move was made solely and cynically in order to score political points, and not because Brendan Nelson or anyone else within the Government really thought those projects presented a genuine problem. This episode was an outright abuse of power, in my view, for its own sake. But strictly speaking Nelson did not overturn designated authority's legitimate decision: the Minister himself was the designated authority.

Regardless of its legality, the veto was a most unwelcome development. Under Iain McCalman's leadership, the Academy had responded to Bolt's earlier contribution by calmly explaining the value of the research he derided, and exposing his method as unprofessional and lightweight (Bolt clearly lacked the diligence to read even the project synopses, relying instead on the titles). Iain gave an upbeat and widely praised National Press Club address, playing on his front foot. We were moderately encouraged by our discussions with the Minister. He publicly repeated his positive noises about the humanities and social sciences, and extended his initial financial support of a new umbrella body (the Council for the Humanities, Arts and Social Sciences or CHASS). On the other hand, we knew that the then ARC CEO, Vicki Sara, had been carpeted in Nelson's office after the Treasurer monstered him, and news had circulated that he wished to establish a star chamber to monitor the College's funding recommendations. But a veto? I don't think anyone in the sector genuinely expected it.

Nevertheless, here we were: Graeme's Presidency started with an unprecedented scandal of political censorship of the humanities, and the ARC's peer review process being undermined by its own Minister. It was as though Graeme had been made for this moment: utterly undaunted, he swung straight into action, his intellectual toolkit immediately deployed in full. He read the complex situation as though it were a controversial box office smash film, circulating in culture and generating meaning as it goes. Without appearing to theorize it consciously, Graeme applied a sophisticated field analysis to this profusion of starkly contradictory signals that were producing a complex interference pattern in the politico-media environment. In retrospect, it is probably just as well there was no time for easing into it: Graeme's instinctive response was precisely the right one, and stepping back to think it through could have been disastrous.

Graeme led the Academy's strategy from the very start with a seemingly instinctive understanding of the stake each player had in the game: the Minister; the columnists; the academics; the ARC; the Academy itself. He had to defend our disciplines, our colleagues, the ARC and the peer review process – and he had to do it pretty much alone, as the other three Academies chose to keep their heads below the parapet, since their own researchers were not affected. CHASS President Malcolm Gillies weighed in with a coordinated response, and a few vice chancellors (university presidents) and leading scientists expressed disquiet, but it was fairly lonely on that soapbox, with little flanking support. The brand new ARC CEO, Peter Høj – who had taken over from Vicki Sara not six months before the veto broke – was in a very difficult position, compounded by the reprehensible abdication of responsibility of his craven Chair, Tim Besley, who was more than happy to throw the humanities to the wolves.

Meanwhile, Graeme's election had disturbed the peace for one of the Prime Minister's favourite historians, Gregory Melleuish, who greeted Graeme's appointment as conclusive evidence of the ending of civilization and the utter capitulation of the scholarly realm to the forces of unbridled left-wing trendiness. The title of his lament says it all: 'Out with Thucydides, in with the Barbie dolls' (Melleuish 2005). Published on 25 February 2005 in *The Australian* (Murdoch's national daily broadsheet), the article ventilated several shared assumptions: that cultural studies is both a symptom and a cause of the degeneracy of humanistic scholarship and artistic practice; that the discipline has no validity, dignity or scholarly relevance; that it is ideologically riven, mired in recondite theory and concerned with the trivial; and that it is the enemy of the proper study of humanity's social and cultural dimensions. Turner's election, according to the author, heralded the arrival of the catastrophe that sensible people like him had been warning us of all along. Now it was too late: the kingdom was lost, the Barbarians had taken the keep. Typically, Melleuish hardly stirred himself to make an argument, holding these truths to be self-evident, confident that his presumed audience already agreed.

In my view, Melleuish's intemperate spray inadvertently revealed that, far from being a disastrous move by the august institution, the election of Turner was a stroke of genius, appointing precisely the right person for the times. The assumptions implied and the accusations manifest in his piece (and others like it around that time) neatly illustrate how perfectly positioned Turner was to defend the humanities from his position as a founder of and senior figure in cultural studies in Australia. As it turned out, his field proved to be an excellent standpoint from which to prosecute the defence of the humanities generally during this period.

The Nelson veto affair was far from the Academy's only concern, but it was a constant presence in our advocacy during that first year of Graeme's Presidency; if only as an example of what can happen if the public abuse of the humanities becomes normalized. Graeme and I took the Academy's concerns about the vetoes and the wider political context to the Minister directly. An affable fellow, he was courteous to a fault whenever we met, and seemed always keen to be liked – even by us. He was polite but firm, insisting that he harboured no antipathy towards the humanities generally, 'not even cultural studies', but that he had simply exercised his grave responsibilities to the parliament and the taxpayer. Graeme attempted to engage him on his concerns with those projects in detail, but the Minister declined to discuss specifics, and instead reiterated his general support.

We addressed our concerns to the senior management of the ARC and its academic advisers, as well as the Secretary of the Department. We discussed it with other members of the government, hoping to gather Party Room support, as well as Senators from smaller parties sitting on the cross benches. We spoke widely with the Opposition, especially the Shadow Minister and Deputy Leader of the Opposition, Jenny Macklin, and one of Labor's most effective interrogators of government in the Senate (later my boss),[2] Senator Kim Carr.

In Opposition, Carr was feared for his forensic scrutiny of officials and Ministers in the Senate Estimates budget review hearings, enabled by his prodigious knowledge and remarkable memory. After coming to Government in 2007, he swiftly impressed as the best-prepared Science Minister in a generation, and his professionalism and loyalty to his officials earned their loyalty in return. He is also a passionate advocate for the humanities and social sciences. An historian by training, a voracious reader of fiction and nonfiction, and a lover of the blues, Carr's rich intellectual life roams deeply into humanities territory.

Carr lives his politics, and he puts his money where his mouth is: his trademark three-piece suits are made by a local fellow he has known for years; he drives an Australian-made car. It is no surprise that his defence of the humanities is instinctive and visceral. For the purposes of the Academy's advocacy on the veto issue and the associated politically supported vilification in the media, it also helped that he had long been a stout defender of academic independence and the sanctity of peer review, and an advocate for the observance of proper process, free from inappropriate political interference. He took up the cudgel against Ministerial over-rule of expert advice, not only in the hope of taking some skin off Nelson, but also as a matter of principle. Carr committed his party to a higher standard: never to exercise a veto for political purposes, and always to give his reasons publicly and fulsomely should there be any other cause to withhold research funding. He lived up to this standard once in government, by never vetoing a grant.

Graeme was walking a very fine line indeed, particularly with the Minister, the Shadow Minister and the ARC CEO. He balanced the forceful communication of a justified indignation with an appreciation of the position in which each of the players found themselves (because this is what determined the possible margins of their responses to his advocacy). He defended the dignity and reputation of our disciplines and the integrity of the peer review process, while protecting the future careers of quite vulnerable researchers and the wellbeing of the diligent ARC staff. He persuaded humanities colleagues to resist gratuitous provocation – and particularly to tone down the rhetorical gestures of performative transgression that had played so precisely into conservative hands – while strengthening the genuine fabric of academic freedom of enquiry. He encouraged the Opposition to see its interest in helping him prosecute the Academy's argument, without alienating the Government, or turning the Academy itself or the humanities generally into a political football.

Just as we had in 2003, the Academy went a few rounds with Bolt in the months following the 2004 veto through the letters page of his own *Herald Sun*, and the Higher Education Supplement (*HES*) of its toney national stablemate, *The Australian*. To their credit, in this and later encounters, these outlets always printed the Academy's responses to direct attacks on humanities researchers. Fanning a continuing debate sells newspapers, of course, but we were also being extended genuine professional courtesy, and perhaps a measure of sympathy in the case of the *HES*.

Following our practice from the year before, Graeme defended particular scholars and projects, but he was also careful to make the general case: that an advanced society conducts research across the board; that you never know where the next valued insight or breakthrough application will come from; that the expert panels know more than journalists, politicians and advisers about the projects; that peer review should always be placed above political expediency; that the research funding system has been refined over time to ensure the greatest rigour and deliver the best value for public funding; that titles tell you little about the nature of a project or the credentials of the researcher; and that the humanities, arts and social sciences have made – and will continue to make – a contribution to our standard of living every bit as valuable and essential as science and technology.

Meanwhile, amidst all this exhausting back-foot play, Graeme was deeply involved in a rather different struggle for recognition and support. Throughout 2005, the four Learned Academies were engaged in a five-yearly review of our joint and several funding program, an exercise that had grown alarmingly from the promised 'light touch' survey to an extended, obsessive-compulsive inquisition worthy of a Royal Commission. The workload was alarming, and it fell very significantly to Graeme to make the case, supported by Iain, the Council and the Secretariat. Graeme, Iain and I ground our way through the review process, spending the whole of the year on a meticulous campaign to convince an impressively unsentimental panel (chaired by the former President of the US National Academy of Sciences, Bruce Alberts, and including the Prime Minister's own hard man, distinguished captain of industry John Ralph) that the Academies represented excellent value for money. At the end of the year, they recommended to the Minister that the Learned Academies ought to have their funding doubled.

In March 2005, Nelson repeated his views on the importance of the humanities at the National Press Club, to a room full of scientists, engineers and technologists assembled for the annual Science Meets Parliament event (Nelson 2005). The Minister repeated his view that their work meant little without the accompanying success of the humanities, arts and social sciences. The assembly did not applaud this gratuitous act of intellectual ecumenicalism: completely unsolicited and easily avoided, it was clearly a genuinely held view that he felt bore repeating. It is also certain that he wanted to throw us a bone, to make some public remarks to mollify a humanities sector offended by the veto affair and the continuing abuse it facilitated in the media. Perhaps he was also trying to split off the wounded outliers while pacifying the herd. If so, he was to be disappointed: the herd was not for turning or for cutting anyone loose.

Not six months into the veto saga, Nelson appointed Iain McCalman to the Prime Minister's Science, Engineering and Innovation Council (PMSEIC), the nation's supreme advisory body on science and research. Originally established in 1977, by 2005 this body comprised the Prime Minister, relevant Ministers and senior officials and leading scientists, engineers and business people. Because of the high access it entailed, considerable prestige accrued to membership. Iain was the first humanities expert ever to be appointed. However belated, this recognition of the nation's need for a humanities perspective at the table was a huge coup, the result of prolonged and dogged lobbying and had immense reputational value. It was also an early and very public manifestation of Graeme's effectiveness and subtlety as an advocate, extracting this historic appointment from the Federal Government while vigorously arguing against the veto.

There were three arguments that all had to be won to achieve this result. It was necessary to convince the Prime Minister and the Minister that expertise in the humanities and social sciences was desirable and useful on the Council; that the current membership's amateur understanding of these fields did not constitute that expertise; and that the right person for the job was someone from the field, rather than one of the government's yes-men. These arguments all met with significant resistance. The laissez-faire economic neoliberals had scant use for the humanities and social sciences, not in the world at large nor on PMSEIC. Many people from the Prime Minister down seemed to consider themselves as well informed on humanities and social science matters as any so-called expert (without the impediment of an actual education in those fields). And the Howard Government had a well-earned reputation for appointing tame fellow-travellers to such positions, and Iain was decidedly not one of those agreeable chaps – if anything, his previous encounters with senior members of the science lobby, in particular, had caused them to regard him with general suspicion and, in one or two cases, open loathing. Countering that, the Government's experience with Iain, as with the Academy generally, had been characterized by honesty and candour, delivered with courtesy and respect. While only those in the Minister's office ever really know the detailed thinking behind these decisions, it seems likely that Graeme's professionalism and Iain's impeccable credentials won the day. It was a considerable coup for Graeme and the Academy.

Although the Academy had engaged the veto debate with some success, and there were positive developments besides, it was of some concern that the right-wing attacks against the humanities continued, both in politics and in the media. An additional worry was Nelson's ostentatious establishment of a community scrutiny committee to examine the ARC's expert recommendations from a point of view of some undefined 'community values'. The committee was a bizarre assembly of a retired judge, a commercial television newsreader and a conservative magazine editor.

However, with all of the positive messages throughout that year – and despite the odd rant from Bolt and his ilk, and the occasional spray from the

ARC community panel's right-wing commentator, Paddy McGuinness – we in the Academy thought that, together with colleagues in the public service and the academic community, we'd had some success in addressing the misconceptions of waste and irrelevance, and had cause for hope that Nelson was ready to defend humanities research, the ARC and the peer review process. He had made some genuinely substantive policy reforms in our favour, which had much more heft than mere sops or gestures. Graeme and I thought that, on balance, the political calculus would counsel against further direct interference.

Reader, we misread him.

When he next had the opportunity in November 2005, the Minister vetoed another batch of humanists, and threw out a couple of social scientists for good measure. This time there were seven projects rejected by the Minister: since one of the new batch had already been vetoed in 2004, the cohort from the two rounds became known as the Nelson Nine. Graeme and the Academy went right back into the fray. This time there was more support from the other Academies and the wider university and research community. Those on the other side of the Ivory Curtain realized that the infection could easily spread to the sciences, should the controversy turn to a scientific topic like stem cell research or climate change.

So the entire cycle repeated, with increased intensity: the tendentious bile of the conservative commentariat; the faux gravitas of the Minister; the scornful vitriol of the Opposition; the hurt and outrage of the humanities community; the expressions of support from ordinary Australians and scholarly types alike; the impressive professionalism of the public servants, especially Høj of the ARC.

Then the Prime Minister chimed in.

On the eve of Australia's national day in late January 2006, Howard gave a nationally televised address to the National Press Club in the Great Hall of Australian Parliament House. About halfway through his speech, he returned to a subject he had made his own over the previous decade: the trouble with history:

> Too often history has fallen victim in an ever more crowded curriculum to subjects deemed more 'relevant' to today. Too often, it is taught without any sense of structured narrative, replaced by a fragmented stew of 'themes' and 'issues'. And too often, history, along with other subjects in the humanities, has succumbed to a postmodern culture of relativism where any objective record of achievement is questioned or repudiated. (Howard 2006)

It is hard to know where to begin with these three astounding sentences, with their conception and articulation so wondrously flawed. Had we but world enough and time, for instance, we could show how the Howard Government's own narrow instrumentalism produced the literalist vocational turn that has infected Australian education at all levels over the past couple of decades, rendering his complaints about 'relevance' a little hypocritical. For our present purpose, let Howard's remarks simply signify the hostility of the government towards a suite of disciplines for which it had no understanding, respect or need. It was a clear expression of support for the attackers in the media like Andrew Bolt, a green light to continue the assault. It may also have been intended as a clarifying signal regarding the veto affair, lest Nelson's promotion to Minister for Defence two days later be misunderstood as a tactical retreat.

Meanwhile, the Review of the Learned Academies Grants Program had gone into a black hole. The Cabinet reshuffle had come just at the crucial moment after the panel delivered its verdict. We had a new Minister, Julie Bishop, who knew little about us, and for whom this review would have been (understandably) a long way down the list of priorities. During the government's internal budget negotiations, a bureaucrat in the Department of Finance took the opportunity to scuttle the Learned Academies' collective finances with the stroke of a red pen. Rumours were confirmed on Budget night 2006, when some extra funding was awarded to CHASS and its science counterpart, but the Academies' position was unchanged.

Having learned how to fight a previous year's battles all over again in the Nelson Veto Saga Parts I and II, Graeme and I ascended our mounting blocks and saddled up again to make the case for Academy funding once more. We engaged in another 12 months of courting the department, the mandarins of the central agencies and a metric plethora of Ministers and backbenchers. Graeme dined with the Minister, in the company of the other Academy Presidents; I dined with the Secretary of the Department of Prime Minister and Cabinet, in the company of the other Academy Executive Directors. We made our cases patiently and comprehensively, and we were heard. The Federal Budget of May 2007 included the funding increase to the Learned Academies that the Alberts report had recommended in 2005. This long campaign, supposedly a light-touch 'check-up' for routine due diligence purposes, had spanned virtually all of Graeme's Presidency, which concluded that November. We had gone out for a morning walk and found ourselves on a long march. Like the veto affair, its pall hung over every other battle or discussion, especially those involving the Department, the Minister and the Parliament.

After all the *Sturm und Drang*, the veto business had ended with a whimper in 2006. In discussions with the new Minister, Graeme had been careful to include his (by now well-polished) arguments against Ministerial interference with an orderly, expert peer review process, and for a broad research enterprise that pursues knowledge across the full range of fields of enquiry. Bishop proved an open-minded and attentive listener. She had proved a capable champion of her portfolio, having secured a dedicated investment fund for educational infrastructure in the 2006 Federal Budget. Bishop put Graeme through his paces – like all effective Ministers, she is tough and sceptical, and as a former litigator she is thorough in her due diligence – but she heard the message, and no doubt appreciated the measured and patient mode of its delivery. At any rate, she had no need to make grand combative gestures, and there were better places for the Government to expend its political capital: there was no use of the veto on her watch.

Politics as scholarly practice

Coming to run a Learned Academy is an intimidating experience for a young scholar (especially one yet to earn his doctorate), populated as it is by titans in your discipline and related fields. When I arrived in August 2003, I was more familiar with the work of Graeme Turner than any other Fellow, largely on account of *Film as Social Practice*, his essential introduction to thinking methodically and multivalently about film and its functions in society and culture. I had relied upon the second edition when writing my honours thesis at Adelaide University on *Blade Runner*, and the third edition continued to be an indispensable guide and reference in the course of my doctoral research at Sydney University. It was one of the spirit guides of my dissertation, texts I kept at my elbow while working. (It remains one of the talismanic books I keep around while writing: I can reach the fourth edition right now from my desk.)

I completed my doctoral thesis during Iain's Presidency, and by the time Graeme became my boss I was under examination. During that antipodean summer of 2004–2005 – while Gregory Melleuish was bemoaning the fall of civilization, and 11 of our compatriots schooled New Zealand and Pakistan in Test cricket – I made the few corrections required of me by my examiners, received the departmental imprimatur, lodged my final copy and waited to graduate. I transferred many of my academic books from home to my office at the Academy, including *Film as Social Practice*.

As 2005 unfolded, I began to reflect on Graeme's style and approach. Iain and I had done great work together, and our effectiveness was partly a function of adaptive compatibility. Graeme and I were just beginning that process, and it was important for me to understand where he was coming from and how he operated, so I could best anticipate, serve and complement him. As it happened, events had conspired to give me an unusually rapid exposure to his *modus operandi* – before he had even had a chance to work it out for himself, perhaps – and it began to ring a bell for me.

Graeme's approach to politics, advocacy, the media and leadership was not only systematic and insightful, but was also based on a sophisticated understanding of institutional power relations, the production of meaning, the multivalency of discursive acts, the iterative nature of production and consumption and the rhizomatic proliferation of signification. His method as President derived from his mastery of the practice of cultural studies. Graeme had taken to the job with an instinctive recourse to a powerful set of interpretive and analytical tools assembled over decades of scholarly practice.

Film as Social Practice offers, for me at least, one window into how this works. Consider this line from the introduction to his fourth edition:

> Film is a social practice for its makers and its audience: in its narratives and meanings we can locate evidence of the ways in which our culture makes sense of itself. Such is the view of film explored through these pages. (Turner 2006a, p. 4)

Just replace a single noun, and Graeme could be outlining his approach to politics. This substitutive approach – politics for film, for instance – provides a compelling and suggestive lens through which to perceive Graeme's approach to the tasks of advocacy and policy advice.

Of course, there is no one-to-one congruence between particular formations in that book – the feature film industry, say – and specific elements in the business of humanities advocacy in the political capital, the national media and the university system. There are many ways one could seek to apply the approach outlined in that volume to Graeme's advocacy method, and each would illuminate in some instances and mislead in others. But I did find a striking resonance between the organization of Graeme's thought in *Film as Social Practice* and the ways I observed him approaching various aspects of his job, with an intellectually rigorous and methodical schema at hand for adaptation.

Equipped with his theoretical sophistication about power and culture, his scholarly engagement with the everyday, and a practiced capacity to defend his field, Graeme's disciplinary perspective and authority gave him some structural advantages that only became apparent as he became immersed in his task of humanities advocacy. But this positioning was only the condition of possibility of effectiveness: it was the manner of his engagement, the way he deployed his scholarly insights and intellectual resources in this new domain, which made him truly effective.

When leaping into the deep end of a big new shark-infested pool, it is unsurprising that people fall back on their existing approaches. There is no gentle start when you come to work in close proximity to politics: you have to just dive in and swim, making do with whatever resources you already have at your disposal. If you are lucky, you find the time and wherewithal to refine your repertoire from there, but people to tend to manifest their origins in the ways they approach the job.

It is unsurprising, then, that Graeme deployed (and then refined) his detailed and deeply analytical approach to cultural studies, when he took on the task of formal advocacy for the humanities at the national level. What is more noteworthy in Turner's engagement inside the Canberra beltway is the methodical and rigorous way he applied his disciplinary grounding to the task.

Graeme's humanities advocacy constitutes, in my view, a remarkable exercise in applied cultural studies, an outstanding demonstration that cultural studies can inform and shape thinking about politics and public value. Indeed, his sophisticated approach was the best demonstration available that cultural studies and the humanities are, *contra* Andrew Bolt, supremely useful.

The afterlife of a chief humanist, 2007–present

As tumultuous as his Presidency had been, Graeme's contribution from November 2004 to November 2007 was only the beginning. In a spooky moment of symmetry, exactly one week after his Presidency finished, the electors of Australia changed the Federal Government. Howard's charmed ride with the electorate had come off the rails with the ascendency of a new Opposition Leader, Kevin Rudd, at the end of 2006. This ushered in a new suite of opportunities for the humanities in Australia. In many ways, our misfortunes in the previous years had come back as boons: to the extent they had been inflicted upon us out of political expediency, the same forces at work had made an ally of the then Opposition, now in Government. But it was much more that this: the incoming Government had nailed its colours to the mast on an array of matters that worked in favour of humanities research. Labor had a mandate to expand research support and opportunity across the disciplines: to increase the overall funding pool and also to remove the constraints excluding the humanities, arts and social sciences. Entire new programs of support were introduced, such as the successful Future Fellowships scheme, open to all. And from Cooperative Research Centres to international research cooperation, schemes that had been cordoned off for the benefit of the sciences alone were opened up to admit the humanities. Again, this had been the result of calm, persistent, sober discussion over the preceding years by the Academy, led by Graeme. But the work of discipline promotion did not finish on election day. To continue to make the case and to support strong humanities proposals, the humanities community needed concerted, well-rehearsed advocacy by trusted, experienced leaders: savvy people to do the heavy lifting once the humanities were allowed to compete.

I do not remember what Graeme Turner did during that week of sweet freedom that ran from the Academy AGM to the Federal Election in November 2007, but I hope that he enjoyed it. No sooner had he vacuumed the sand from the floor of his car than he was summoned back into the fray. Typically, he responded immediately and professionally to the call. Before he knew it, Graeme was everywhere: leading the national argument for a dedicated research infrastructure program for the HASS sector; riding shotgun in numerous delegations, providing counsel on appointments and policy reforms; ensuring the humanities were properly treated in the design of the new national research assessment exercise; and being appointed to PMSEIC himself.

The new Government commissioned a 2008 review of the National Collaborative Research Infrastructure System. Graeme was appointed chair of the Humanities, Arts and Social Sciences Expert Working Group: it was an enormous commitment of time and energy, but there were serious indications that humanities requirements would – finally – be taken seriously in discussions of infrastructure funding. At the same time, Graeme completed a scoping study on the development of a national scholarly digital archive in the humanities, a project which had originated with the previous Coalition Minister, Julie Bishop, and which had the support of the new Labor Minister, Kim Carr. He continued his engagement with the Excellence in Research for Australia initiative, not only chairing the subcommittee advising on indicators of research quality in the humanities, but also leading the humanities scrutiny of the first trail round.

Graeme continued his close involvement in the development of the many policy submissions undertaken by the Academy, on issues as diverse as the future of the book industry, research training, national cultural policy and higher education funding. At the time of writing, Graeme has just delivered yet another high-level policy project, Mapping the Humanities and Social Sciences, a collaboration of the Academies of Humanities and Social Sciences, the Office of the Chief Scientist, and the Department of Industry (into which the science portfolio was subsumed under the new Abbott Coalition Government when it won power in September 2013).

It is fitting that Graeme was finally elevated to PMSEIC, because it captures nicely the altitude at which his advocacy for our common cause has operated all this time. It is representative in other ways, too, of the working conditions of much of Graeme's time inside the beltway, behind those closed doors: working more or less alone; well briefed up to a point but flying on instinct after that; surrounded by people who don't entirely get the humanities, and who rely upon us in ways they don't really understand or even recognize; forming unlikely alliances and friendships; and handling with patience the familiar suspicion and hostility of the uncomprehending.

Graeme's position on PMSEIC survived a radical trimming of that body in 2012 chiefly because of the regard in which his experience, judgement and intelligence were held by the Prime Minister, the Science and Research Minister and the Chief Scientist. However, in October 2014, PMSEIC was wound up by the new conservative government, to be replaced by a Science Council comprising science and technology leaders and the captains of industry. The new structure spurns the input of social and cultural expertise. It is the Old Firm, reinstated by a government that did not even have a Science Minister, let alone an interest in what makes people tick. In some respects, the humanities, arts and social sciences seem to be back where we were a decade ago: perhaps Nietzsche had a point. This blow came just as Graeme was about to launch his project mapping the humanities and social sciences in Australia. The timing is both ironic and revelatory. It certainly captures the difficult environment in which Graeme has operated, his determination and will, and his continuing relevance even to power structures that would prefer to ignore our fields. This testifies to the exemplary contribution for the national benefit of our friend, colleague and inspiration, Graeme Turner, through a decade of dogged, intelligent, effective application of keen native wit and deep disciplinary insight to his various formal roles of national advocacy for the humanities.

Disclosure statement

No potential conflict of interest was reported by the authors.

Notes

1 This account was related to me by a politician present at the time. A version later narrated in my presence by a senior official who had also been in the room largely accords.
2 I served two stints in government as Senior Adviser in Carr's Ministerial office (May 2010 to January 2012 and July–October 2013), responsible for science, research, higher education and book industry policy.

References

Bolt, A. (2003) 'Grants to grumble', *Herald Sun*, 19 November, p. 19.
Bolt, A. (2004) 'Paid to be pointless', *Herald Sun*, 26 November, p. 18.

Carr, K. (2013) *A Letter to Generation Next: Why Labor*, Melbourne, Melbourne University Press.

Commonwealth of Australia (2001) *Australian Research Council Act 2001*, http://www.comlaw.gov.au/Series/C2004A00773 (accessed 13 October 2014).

English, D. (2003) '$450,000 to study mobile phone', *Sunday Mail*, 9 November, p. 13.

Haigh, G. (2006) 'The Nelson Touch', *The Monthly*, May, http://www.themonthly.com.au/issue/2006/may/1294984634/gideon-haigh/nelson-touch (accessed 13 October 2014).

Howard, J. (2006) 'A sense of balance: The Australian achievement in 2006', Australia Day Address to the National Press Club, Great Hall, Australian Parliament House, Canberra, 25 January, http://pmtranscripts.dpmc.gov.au/browse.php?did=22110 (accessed 13 October 2014).

McCalman, I. (2004) Making Culture Bloom, National Press Club Address, with an introduction by Malcolm Gillies, Canberra, Council of Humanities, Arts and Social Sciences (CHASS), http://www.chass.org.au/speeches/SPE200406 16IM.php (accessed 13 October 2014).

Melleuish, G. (2005) 'Out with Thucydides, in with the Barbie dolls', *The Australian*, http://www.theaustralian.com.au/common/story_page/0,5744,12360865%255E7583,00.html (accessed 25 February).

Nelson, B. (1999) *Health in the Ideal World: Medicine in Valhalla*, The Sir Herbert Maitland Oration, University of Sydney, 26 October, http://www.adf.com.au/archive.php?doc_id=23 (accessed 13 October 2014).

Nelson, B. (2003) 'Minister for Education, Science and Training Federal Budget Media Release', 13 May.

Nelson, B. (2005) 'Science meets parliament address', *National Press Club, Canberra*. 8 March, http://webarchive.nla.gov.au/gov/20050723010953/http://dest.gov.au/Ministers/Media/Nelson/2005/03/ntran080305.asp (accessed 15 October 2014).

Presidents' Reports (2003–2010) Annual Proceedings of the Australian Academy of the Humanities, www.humanities.org.au.

Turner, G. (2006a). *Film as Social Practice*, 4th edn, Oxford and New York, NY, Routledge (1st ed., 1988; 2nd, 1993; 3rd ed., 1999).

Turner, G. (2006b) 'Informing the public: Is there a place for a critical humanities?' Proceedings of AAH Annual Lecture 2005, Canberra, Australian Academy of the Humanities, pp. 131–141.

Melissa Gregg

THE EFFECTIVE ACADEMIC EXECUTIVE

As Director of the Centre for Critical and Cultural Studies at the University of Queensland from 2000–2012, Graeme Turner led one of the longest running research investments in Cultural Studies' history. Holding these threads together, in conjunction with the sheer hard work of Centre affiliates and administrators, was an exemplary management style. Turner's brand of Cultural Studies is defined by an attention to the art and politics of management alongside the customary business of doing research. It is Cultural Studies' lack of engagement with management theory that has made this type of work difficult to appreciate, even while it is just this kind of engagement that is necessary to ensure the survival of the field. Acknowledging the significance of Turner's management politics, its relevance to his broader intellectual project, and its importance for the field of Cultural Studies more broadly, this paper pays tribute to a leader whose career demands a more nuanced vocabulary for institutional work within and outside the university.

As Director of the Centre for Critical and Cultural Studies (CCCS) at the University of Queensland from 2000–2012, Graeme Turner led one of the longest running research investments in Cultural Studies' history. Countless numbers of students, researchers and administrators benefited from this effort, and as a research fellow at the Centre from 2004–2008, I am one of them. The CCCS is a unique organizational accomplishment in Australian academia. Its open intellectual mandate fostered a new generation of internationally regarded scholars in areas as varied as Asia-Pacific popular culture, Internet studies, cultural history, anthropology, media studies, critical theory, disability studies, science and technology studies and international communication. Holding these threads together, in conjunction with the sheer hard work of the Centre's affiliates and administrators, has been Turner's exemplary management style. His role as a mentor and keen institutional operator is a combination as crucial as it is rare. Turner's brand of Cultural Studies is defined by an attention to the art and politics of management alongside the customary business of doing research. It is Cultural Studies' lack of engagement with management theory that has made this type of work difficult to appreciate.

The political registers that have dominated the field often show suspicion if not outright indignation towards the business of administration and management. This allergic reaction constitutes an anti-intellectualism that at times rivals the very snobbery Cultural Studies initially set out to oppose.[1] To begin to improve this situation, and create a more nuanced vocabulary for institutional work within and outside the university, this paper acknowledges the significance of Turner's management politics, its relevance to his broader intellectual project and its importance for the field of Cultural Studies more broadly.

Cultural Studies' aversion to management theory is surprising given its impact on universities, which stand as the key location of practice for the field. Critical analysis of management discourse largely takes place in Business Schools and the discipline of Organizational Studies, with its own rigorous tradition of publication. Emerging subfields such as Critical Management Studies, and theories of organization from a worker's perspective (the journal *ephemera* or conferences like Computer Supported Cooperative Work) often show affinities with the labourist traditions typical of early (British) Cultural Studies, even if scholars are not often in contact with each other. Management theory is of course part of the broader landscape for criticism in analyses of university life more generally, from Bill Readings' (1997) *The University in Ruins* to Mary Evans' (2004) *Killing Thinking*. If these publications address the consequences of management practices on the university institution as a whole, Cultural Studies remains overdue for a mode of engagement that is fitting the experience of our discipline and its strengths.

Those closest to accounts of management theory I am seeking typically identify as sociologists, whether in the case of Paul Du Gay's (2000) defence of bureaucracy or Nigel Thrift's *Knowing Capitalism* (2005). In different ways, these writers identify the structural transformations taking place in knowledge institutions over the course of several decades. Both recognize that changes to organizations necessarily involve changes to people, and the kinds of subjectivities that are valued and rewarded by formal incentives. Building on these efforts, I want to extend this principle to outline some of the benefits of a more substantial engagement with management theory in Cultural Studies. Following Turner's example, as managers Cultural Studies academics can regard their work in the university as part of a broader ethics, one that puts service to the field on equal footing with individual research progress. This is an important strategy of accumulation, consolidation and defence in the face of growing tendencies towards auditing and accountability that pit academics against each other. In addition, I suggest that as scholars, Cultural Studies academics might use their technical skills to produce a more aggressive response to the mandates underwriting their experience, to question common-sense thinking. The more open form of address I will advocate below is intended to bring transparency to the sometimes overly inflated and fantastical discourses of efficiency and impact that are applied to university work.

The occasion of a festschrift offers a moment to assess what is at stake in any discipline. For Cultural Studies, a reluctance to engage critically and coherently with management theory and practice risks a naiveté in the forms of institutional politics that are required to ensure there is a field to defend in years to come. A certain blindness to the idea of treating scholarly work *as work* is one factor that prevents much reflexivity amongst academics implicated in wider structural forces that clearly include managerial trends (Gill 2009, Gregg 2009a, 2011). As Andrew Ross (2000) argued over a decade ago, academics' 'sacrificial labour' provides a useful model upon which the exploitation of discounted labour in other creative industries can be legitimated. Today, it is the content as much as the temporality of labour that constitutes academics' contribution to the knowledge economy. 'Knowing capitalism' depends on ever greater transfer and traffic between public and private research institutions. As Thrift (2005, p. 33) convincingly argues, 'social theory now has a direct line to capitalism': this is simply the business of innovation in the global economy and the university's role therein. But what would it mean to bring the theories of capitalism to the attention of Cultural Studies, to reverse this move? What critical insights might flow from a direct encounter with the popular pedagogy of management?[2]

Many readers will note that my title borrows from the 1966 book, *The Effective Executive,* by the icon of management theory, Peter Drucker. One of the world's leading 'management gurus' (Huczynski 2006), Drucker epitomizes the can-do ethos of corporate America and a genre of motivational business thinking dating back at least as far as the Depression. Drucker's advice in *The Effective Executive* captures techniques of entrepreneurial self-management suited to new kinds of professionals navigating the instability of work in large corporations (Kanter 1993). The book's opening lines are a memorable reflection of its simple premise:

> Whether he works in a business or in a hospital, in a government agency or in a labour union, in a university or in the army, the executive is, first of all, expected to *get the right things done*. And this is simply saying that he is expected to be effective. (Drucker 1966, p. 1)

This passage isolates the unique qualities of the superior manager: the results-oriented executive. It also captures many of the expectations bestowed upon Turner by colleagues, as I will illustrate in more detail shortly. Drucker rode the wave of publishing and marketing opportunity that emerged in tandem with the rise of the corporation and the growing discipline of management studies. In the barrage of self-help publishing that accompanied the growth of this influential class, Drucker is simply the tip of the iceberg, part of a billowing genre of extra-curricular guidance. These manuals for time- and self-management were the domestic variety of management theories championed in more formal avenues and teaching institutions, from scientific management to human relations, to theories of chaos and flux (Crainer and Dearlove 1999, Thrift 2005). Drucker's symbolic role in the broader repertoire of post-Fordist business practice is immense. Focusing specifically on the mindset of the manager, he offered the tools and reassurance to prove that 'effectiveness can be learned'. These maxims served as popular counsel for a generation of newly minted middle-managers seeking viable authority and tactics as much as a paycheck. Recognizing this history is useful background for understanding the kinds of professional subjectivity taken for granted in universities today, and the modes of performance that are taken as common sense.

My recourse to Drucker is intended as a gesture to suit a Cultural Studies approach to management, given that the field has always taken popular phenomena as generative of vernacular theory. In the case of Graeme Turner's formative work (e.g. Turner 1986, Fiske *et al.* 1987, Turner and Tulloch 1990), this is especially the case – as we will see, the battle to secure the viability of teaching popular culture provided much of Turner's early university experience. Bringing Cultural Studies traditions and methods to bear on management theory recognizes the industrial significance of their precepts as much as their ideological function. As du Gay writes:

> these discourses of work reform arise in specific political contexts, and have potential consequences, but they are not merely functional responses to, or legitimations of, already existing economic interests or needs. Rather than simply reflecting a pre-given social world, they themselves actively 'make up' a social reality and create new ways for people to be at work. (du Gay in Thrift 2005, p. 39)

Against this version of reality, this essay combines Drucker's advice to readers with classic mentoring tips from Turner that have proven routinely useful in my own career. This fusion of academic and business history with 'anecdotal theory' (Gallop 2002, Morris 2006) is offered as one response to the complex forces affecting employee subjectivity in this phase of capitalism. Cultural Studies' methods are characteristically partial (Frow and Morris 1993). Invoking the personal alongside an account of management theory provides empirical context for and materiality to the various pressures faced by academics. It also points to shifts in organizational behaviour that have taken place as ideals of professional instruction suited to a pre-Internet bureaucratic life (and Cultural Studies' institutional beginnings) give way to the chronically connected, hyper-informed, data determined workplaces of the present. It is these conditions that pose new kinds of threat to academic practice, whether it is at the level of our minds or bodies (Barcan 2013) or the ideas of civic good that drove Cultural Studies in the past. It is in these fraught circumstances that scholars must continue to find an operational ethics and for which Turner's career offers an instructive example.

The poverty of management theory

Cultural Studies' aversion to management theory is understandable within the field's British lineage, which always had a distinct anti-capitalist bent.[3] Figures like Raymond Williams balanced the radicalism of projects like the *May Day Manifesto* with the established traditions of Trinity College, following formative teaching experiences in Workers Education Association classes. Intellectuals of the first New Left – EP Thompson (1978) and Perry Anderson (1980) among them – famously argued over *any* engagement with theory as the appeal of Althusserian Marxism took hold. Suggesting that Cultural Studies should engage with the tenets of management might therefore appear as a perverse extension of this heritage. To tease out this possibility further, though, we can discern an alternative path for a Cultural Studies of management if we place Turner in sympathy with another British Cultural Studies pioneer, Richard Hoggart, author of *The Uses of Literacy* (1957) and founder of the Birmingham Centre for Contemporary Cultural Studies (BCCCS). Hoggart brokered the initial investment from Sir Allen Lane of Penguin Books that led to the establishment of the Centre with additional funding from Chatto and *The Observer* (Lee 2003, p. 75). Moving to Birmingham to take a Professorship of Modern English Literature, Hoggart cited a sense of responsibility to create an institutional foundation for the values espoused in his groundbreaking book. Directorship of the BCCCS only moved to Stuart Hall when Hoggart moved to Paris for a position with UNESCO. Factoring in his later stint as Warden of Goldsmiths College, Hoggart's career is a portrait of public service. His life's work enacted a belief in defending the dignity and empathy of working-class people, the universal right to a cultural and intellectual life (Owen 2008).

There are few better descriptions of a bureaucratic worldview than that contained in the title of Hoggart's memoir of his time at UNESCO, *An Idea and its Servants* (1978). Turner's record of institutional work fits this mold, albeit with a distinctly antipodean bent. His experiences as a student in Australia, the UK and Canada established a belief in a public service model of education and a vision of university life with little nostalgia for the aristocracy of the sandstone campus.[4] As an academic, Turner's management style fused the service ethos of the bureaucrat with the performance emphasis of the executive. He took seriously the responsibilities of office, especially in the roles that came later in his career: as CCCS Director, President of the Australian Academy of the Humanities and leader of the Australian Research Council (ARC) Cultural Research Network. Each of these leadership positions carried an interest in regenerating the disciplinary areas with which Turner shared allegiance. They ensured the material and affective infrastructure necessary to support a continuing community of scholars. At a time of success for Cultural Studies and other New Humanities disciplines, Turner focused on the long game. Securing funding was only the start of the job: the further step was to see every victory as a bastion to be guarded and defended from later attack. When many Cultural Studies academics took the critique of neoliberal economics as a priority – its impact on funding for universities serving as just cause – indeed, at a time when working with government was out of favour with his peers (see Frow 2006), Turner's determined dialogue with management advanced the organizational front needed to win institutional space for others. While aspects of his style were certainly unique (his fondness for colourful language being one), the amount of effort Turner dedicated to improving and finessing the skills needed to advance Cultural Studies' success should not be underestimated. Following Drucker, this work can be regarded as the discipline of learning to be *effective*.

Life at the CCCS, or, how to be a research manager

> The effective executive focuses on contribution. He looks up from his work and outward towards goals. He asks: What can I contribute that will significantly affect the performance and the results of the institution I serve? His stress is on responsibility. (Drucker 1966, p. 54)

According to Drucker (1966, pp. 24–25), effective executives:

- know where their time goes
- focus on outward contribution
- build on strengths
- concentrate on the few major areas where superior performance will produce outstanding results
- make effective decisions.

Turner illustrated all of these qualities as CCCS Director. Time management, for instance, was his true forte. Few people would be able to remember Graeme ever being late for anything. Punctuality is a deceptive skill. It is a measure of leadership to be able to protect others from knowledge of the many competing demands on one's time. Graeme maintained a remarkable rate of publication and grant-based success throughout the CCCS years – key measures of his 'outward contribution' – in addition to the many roles he occupied for the university. Yet he always had time for a friendly chat when it was needed. As junior scholars, struggling to balance the new expectations and duties expected of us, Graeme gave us simple techniques to stay on course, including pragmatic advice on how to say no and decline offers politely. The phrase: 'I'm sorry, I'm fully committed' is the elusive and magical sentence he introduced to me early on, as a simple default response to an impossible request. It was only later that I would learn just how few academics seemed capable of imagining such a statement.

Graeme's tips for navigating meetings were another revelation. They included establishing pre-determined departure times and communicating them with organizers in advance (even if the reason for departing may have been a slight distortion!). 'Getting the right things done' (Drucker 1966, p. 1) meant taking a ruthless approach to pure administrative process. Avoiding time-sapping meetings required deliberate strategies: ordering agenda items according to importance, working behind the scenes before the event, and being prepared to walk out of conversations that veered from accomplishing goals.

In the CCCS itself, the secret to ongoing success was to 'concentrate on the few major areas where superior performance will produce outstanding results'. This is one way to explain the substantial publishing record and grant-winning success the Centre enjoyed for over a decade. Like its neighbour in the Forgan Smith Tower – the Centre for the History of European Discourses the CCCS punched above its weight in terms of funding acquired and spent. Put another way, the Centre operated according to the Human Resources truism: 'people are our most valuable asset'. Researchers were not required to uphold Graeme's personal intellectual project. Fellows were selected based on the quality of their work on merit, regardless of theoretical or disciplinary specialty. The freedom to explore and compose a path of one's own made the Centre a highly supportive and unique environment. Without the mandate of a singular conceptual agenda or programme, it was not surprising that colleagues referred to my workplace as simply 'Graeme's Centre'. The perception that Graeme was the driving force is a reflection of the personal interest he took in establishing the institution and close working relationships with those who joined it. Once Graeme decided to support someone, it was really only a matter of faculty politics as to whether the person was funded. Of course, it is the point of this paper to explain why, when these battles were fought, so many times he won.

Graeme's leadership had multiple benefits. As an experienced university administrator, he protected postdoctoral scholars from the currents of institutional pressure, separating the research experience from the logistical work of reporting, lobbying and leadership. He created a space for sympathetic collegiality, an experience best captured in the simple format of the monthly staff meeting. In these get-togethers, administrators, junior researchers and professors all shared updates, opinions and DIY catering, making matters of hierarchy and status temporarily irrelevant. Graeme enacted in these gestures his own egalitarian hopes for the university as a community of democratic participation. It would only occur to me many years later, in international universities with far greater capacities to bestow rewards on the highly ranked, that I realized the significance of this perspective. The God Professor of the Anglo-American academy would rarely lower himself to the trivia of organizing tea and biscuits.

The CCCS enabled a privileged group of scholars a cocoon from the more contentious and messy reality of academic and departmental politics.

The Centre's research-only mandate put emphasis on value for money: contracts of three to four years were timed to capitalize on the productivity and ambition of researchers at the early stage of their career. These positions allowed precious time for experimentation and the refinement of ideas needed to generate useful, topical research. The CCCS gave support and space for scholars to consolidate their viability in an increasingly demanding outside job market. If this protection had downsides, however, it was that few of us had enough exposure to the full assault of institutional politics that would take place in the inevitable transition to other jobs. Our time as postdocs separated us physically and intellectually from the classroom conditions of teaching, for instance, and some of the larger changes to academic labour affecting others.[5] The difference in working locations was more than just a question of pace – how to juggle teaching in relation to writing and fieldwork – it was also a matter of reconfiguring access and availability to a much larger pool of people. Research fellows are encouraged to believe that writing is the main route available to prove their worth to an audience or a public. As a teacher, indeed in almost any other knowledge profession, the reality of a job's impact is more localized. The audience for your ideas comes down to earth.[6]

Leaving the Centre meant coming to terms with a teaching and research environment defined by new technologies of availability. In my experience, this included catching on to a constant stream of communication from students and co-workers through email, online courseware and social media. Colleagues who were largely invisible in corridors or offices would have no trouble emailing endless amounts of requests, updates and messages at all times of the day and night. Meanwhile, those with whom I shared most day-to-day contact were non-continuing, contract-dependent students and administrators. These were dear colleagues, to be sure, and their contribution to the delivery of undergraduate teaching was essential to the success of the department. I found it hard to reckon with the reality that these talented young professionals worked such long hours in course organization, student counselling, preparation and evaluation but had little say in shaping the curriculum, or developing the long-term identity of a department or school. The phantom of job security haunted their efforts.[7] For all of us, teaching administration meant keeping abreast of a myriad of tasks imposed by automated deadlines and reminder bots from software packages designed to normalize screen-based interaction. These systems worked together to create a scenario where even face-to-face teaching involved obligatory and repetitive online content, optimized for remote consumption (McKay and Brass 2011).

Ad hoc academics

The decade in which the CCCS first flourished, then, coincided with key management tendencies that affected the material work of Cultural Studies.

The uptake of new communication technologies, the intensification of productivity measures, the packaging of higher education for an international export market and the embrace of interdisciplinarity are just some of these decisions that impacted the character of university life and teaching. The growing numbers of Ph.D. graduates available as a cheap labour pool set up a parasitic relationship between employers seeking to deliver courses flexibly and workers whose insecure positions fostered compliance. The further effect of this split in responsibility for undergraduate instruction was the acceleration of performance metrics for teaching, research and service, with consequences for their possible compatibility.

Ruth Barcan (2013) usefully describes this setting as a 'palimpsest' university: an institution operating as a vaguely corresponding copy of its original vision; a finite shell of its former self. On the surface, the academic professoriate continues to embody the hopes and traditions of higher education, but a fundamental tension exists between the scholarly and corporate ethos espoused by management. 'The servant of too many masters', Barcan writes, 'academics must not only submit themselves to the exigencies of each regime' but also 'maintain life in a number of different systems simultaneously' (Barcan 2013, p. 121). It 'is not so much that a new paradigm has succeeded an older one', but that academics are 'trying to uphold the values and practices of an older regime at the same time' (Barcan 2013). Academics are thus invited to take individual responsibility for smoothing out the contradictions inherent to large, bureaucratic organizations. Successful employees are those able to become self-managing subjects, or what I term, drawing from Jencks and Silver (2013/1972), 'ad hoc' professionals.

Ad hoc professionals use what is to hand to cobble together the affective and technical infrastructure for career continuity and success. These highly qualified but precariously employed workers engage in expansive forms of immaterial labour (Gorz 2010). These off-the-clock, self-sought and self-taught strategies are targeted at producing a professional subjectivity able to withstand the management requirement for 'flexibility'. If the shift to performative professionalism is central to 'the new spirit of capitalism' (Boltanski and Chiappello 2005), it is especially prevalent in the world of contemporary academia, where the autonomous work culture long cherished by tenured faculty often leads to irregular hours with few defined limits. In the context of highly mediated work worlds, however, where collegiality is so often defined by presence in an inbox, this experience has the potential to be intensely individual (Gregg 2011). For academics, the combined impact of non-continuing jobs, online course offerings, remote work and management by email is the psychological challenge posed by ad hoc professionalism.

As Barcan (2013, p. 113) notes of academia: 'we have witnessed a shift from an era where professionalism meant that one could be trusted to one in which professionalism means that one is obliged to provide regular *evidence* of one's activity and one's competence'.

> Not only do we do our work, we also do substantial forms of 'meta-work' (Fisher 2011, p. 127), such as asking for work (e.g. grant applications); creating and maintaining the conditions in which to do work (learning new software; dealing with computer problems; technical in-servicing); reporting on work (to our managers, to the government, to external stakeholders); updating our public profile; and undertaking other forms of professional development (e.g. mandatory courses on equity in the workplace, intercultural sensitivity and so on). (Barcan 2013, p. 125)

This 'hyperemployment' (Bogost 2013) risks becoming an all-consuming project for today's aspiring professionals, leaving little energy or 'hope' for the alternative work and lifestyles Barcan endorses. As Turner (2012, p. 172), acknowledges, in the final pages of *What's Become of Cultural Studies?*, this has particular significance for young people entering the industry:

> new academics are often given unrealistic targets for their output and their impact; they are required to become well published almost immediately upon completing the apprenticeship of the PhD; and the oppression of the performance indicator or the unpredictability of the tenure process requires them to continually monitor their progress in ways their predecessors rarely had to do, let alone at such an early stage in their careers. Senior academics in the field have a duty of care to these young people to provide advice and mentoring so that they might successfully manage their relation to their institution. In general, there is not a lot of evidence that this duty has either been accepted or discharged. Largely, the young researcher is left to deal with their anxieties alone. (Turner 2012)

Turner's take on the competitive nature of the high-performance university is welcome recognition of the changing circumstances for Cultural Studies' practice. It is further evidence of the need to understand the management principles serving to encourage and reward particular subjective states within organizations. One way of approaching this is to consider the difference between today's measures for professional relevance and those of Cultural Studies' beginnings. Turner offered just this kind of history lesson in a keynote address to the *State of the Industry* conference in Sydney in 2009 – an occasion when the working conditions for cultural research took centre stage. In an effort to assuage the career angst of his young colleagues, and in a gesture that underscored the shared concern that this vital network for sharing experience and research across generations was coming to an end, Turner took the uncharacteristic move of offering his own experience as evidence in his remarks. I quote these details at some length here, as this speech has never been published:

I took my first academic job in 1971. I was 24. When I started, I was not asked to undergo performance appraisals or report against key performance indicators, raise interest in my research from industry partners or end users, submit research grant applications, address university requirements for community engagement, set out a research program, or indeed publish. Universities were not businesses, they were organized around disciplinary departments, and salaries had just been boosted by the Whitlam government. Over the first three years of my academic career my salary trebled.

I was, though, teaching 16 hours a week in a CAE where very few of the staff had active research interests and where the delivery of the teaching program was the only thing on anybody's mind. The disciplines in which I was later to build my career – cultural and media studies – did not exist. Until they did, I was told that I could do research in these areas if I wanted, but I could not teach in them. Those of my colleagues who had completed a PhD more or less stopped researching after that was done. (Turner 2009, n.p.)

This passage is emblematic of Turner in its modest attention to empirical details. Any benefits he enjoys as a new academic are placed in cultural and historical context, with salaries and research guidelines linked to government policy and fluctuations in management practice. The priorities for Cultural Studies practice could hardly have changed more with the passing of time. For today's wanna-be academics, the Ph.D. is only the beginning of a lifelong exercise in research performance. A 'career' is less a carriage through the stages of life, as in the original meaning of the term, but an effort to build reliable correlations between the expectation of ongoing employment and the stylistic illustration of activity. In documents that attend funding and promotion applications, researchers are only as good as their last three years. Incentive structures pivot on proving excellence across teaching, research and service roles. In the national funding pool, publication activity is quantified by timeliness as much as disciplinary impact. Researchers cannot trade-off past glories or become complacent in their achievements.

There is much to lament about these changes, but Turner's reflections give us pause for consideration. The fact that the imperatives for demonstrable academic success have changed so much in the course of a few decades is proof that with further changes in management fashion, these measures will only change again. What's more, in the long view regularly adopted by Turner, one can acknowledge the substantial accomplishment that there are now Cultural Studies grant categories to apply for, and teaching and research jobs that provide the possibility of employment. It was Turner's generation that turned these previously inconceivable opportunities into expectations for others.

The larger concern for Cultural Studies is the extent to which the field has become 'among the Humanities disciplines where everyday practice has become increasingly professionalized, strategic and institutionally oriented' (Turner 2012, p. 172). For Turner (2012, p. 10), 'the principles of privatization, entrepreneurialism and individualism are anathema ... to cultural studies thinking' since they threaten the Humanities' role of producing skills and qualities directed towards defending the public good for its own sake. If some elements of neoliberal economic reform have been less problematic for Turner – the growing number of accountability instruments applied to scholarly work, for instance – this is because they can be used to show evidence of Cultural Studies' impact and success. Among Humanities academics, Turner has been a vocal supporter of methods that can help to demonstrate the value of Cultural Studies research, especially in relation to more established disciplines that traditionally traded cultural cache for patronage. Among other things, the rise of audit culture enabled powerful claims for resources.

Spending time with 'The Suits' did not come naturally to Graeme. He dislikes corporate culture's macho self-importance as much as he hates the ostentatious elitism of the traditional university. He is typically unimpressed by overt trappings of power and as CCCS Director he minimized participation in 'after hours' networking events that mixed business with leisure. This latter was partly a hangover from his time as a Chair of the Department of English, where avoiding the wrath of angry colleagues was a necessary form of self-defence. But it was also an example to others that it is possible to reject parts of corporate culture that do not conform to personal principles.

Engaging with management *thinking* was however a key part of Turner's armoury of perseverance, empathy and foresight in shaping a research and disciplinary agenda. This sophisticated political manoeuvring has often been misrecognized as simple advocacy or government lobbying at best, a surrender to administration at worst. An alternative view is to see this as a multifaceted engagement with the instruments of control in a managerial culture focused solely on results. Turner bore witness to new modes of management in his rise through the ranks of the university. Taking these changes seriously meant coming to terms with the challenge of providing evidence to protect himself and others as the rules of the game changed. Turner's attention to the art of management enabled him to be proactive as a research leader – always looking to be on the front foot – meeting the touchstones for performance required of a university governed by shifting metrics for 'excellence' (Readings 1997).

The rules of the game

At each university, at each stage of his teaching and research career, Turner embarked on the dogged political work of figuring out the levers to power and where these were open for debate. As he relates in interview:

I've perhaps been more naturally interested in how the structures in the university system work, how they change, what they enable when they change, and how to work the system to make use of what it enables each time. And in my case, I really needed to know this stuff because *every* job I took involved setting up cultural studies from scratch in an institution that didn't really want it, and where there was no space for it. So the politics of that are institutional politics. And I just got pretty good at it, I guess, because I did it so many times (Turner in King 2010, pp. 152–153).

These comments highlight the variations of power and agency that are available within large organizations if management is taken as a legitimate outlet for political acumen. They show how Cultural Studies techniques – of identifying sources of power, of searching for openings – can be used to advance an agenda. As Turner elaborates:

I like seeing how the political power works in an institution and then seeing how you can make it work for you. I haven't set out to become the Vice Chancellor or anything like that. I don't find *that* interesting. I'm not interested in a career in administration; I'm interested in how the system works so I can use it. Ever since I decided Cultural Studies was my main interest, my project really has been to develop it in Australia and protect its interests once it was developed. That's what I've done. (Turner in King 2010, pp.152–153)

For an international audience, this helps to situate the significance of Turner's political battles on campus, and the sheer will that drove his engagement with management structures of the university. Turner pressed the cause for Cultural Studies from the ground up: it was a local political practice that responded to the needs of his field and his colleagues in periods of persistent institutional pressure (see Byron 2015). While it was not a role he sought – Turner maintains a healthy Australian disdain for the stuffy elitism he perceives in the role of 'Vice Chancellor' and the like – it is a duty to which he responded given the needs of the field and the principles he sought to maintain. The role of bureaucrat came naturally because of his unwavering belief in the value of the university as a public good.

That Turner did this while management trends were moving swiftly to enshrine the logic of competitive individualism is a compelling and – in Barcan's (2013) terms – *hopeful* story. For every success Graeme enjoyed that may have been seen as a personal accomplishment, there were always opportunities for others attached. This has been a feature of his recent role as a Federation Fellow at the University of Queensland, which attracted multiple postdoctoral positions for young scholars, and was a notable strength of the ARC Cultural Research Network Turner led for five years from 2005–2009. One of the reasons Turner continues to be so fondly admired, I suggest, is that his victories have tended to translate as collective triumphs. Turner's ability to deliver results at both ends of the academic political spectrum – the level of institutional influence and the sharing of winnings upon success – has been an effective counter the individualizing dimensions enshrined in the performance management measures favoured by university administrators.

In praise of organization

For Cultural Studies to deny the role of management in determining its fate is to accept a certain hysteria over the question of organization.[8] It omits recognition of the field's ultimate endorsement by many universities as much as it shirks responsibility for maintaining investment in a project that would prefer to consider itself radical. 'Once our place in the higher education establishment has been secured ... it becomes implausible to continue to indulge in fantasies of our independence from that formulation' Turner writes (2012, p. 66). Avoiding outright confrontation with management discourse has led to a separation between Cultural Studies' theory and everyday practice. Disappointingly, given the field's history, it has often meant a purely tactical approach to labour politics: a culture of complaint and withdrawal, a decline in union activism and a process of inward retreat and isolation.

Turner's willingness to contest and negotiate management dictates is a mode of professional perseverance only few contemporaries in Australian Cultural Studies have matched or followed.[9] As I have implied, this reluctance is partly due to the changing nature of academic employment, where the experience of collegiality is placed under strain by short-term contracts, competition for security and results-oriented resource rewards. If university managers move their core business from the provision of higher education as a civic service, Turner's style of bureaucratic manoeuvring will prove difficult to replicate in future. But his example shows that a corporate emphasis and an engagement with management are not necessarily detrimental to Cultural Studies' renewal and continued flourishing.

As Drucker (1966, p. 57) explains, 'every organization needs performance in three major areas: it needs direct results; building of values and their reaffirmation; and building and developing people for tomorrow'. In Turner, Cultural Studies benefited from a leader who excelled across these three areas. His work was consistently results-oriented, both in his own research and in the advice he gave to others. His belief in the value of the university played out in his indefatigable service and in the areas he chose to publish and comment. His stewardship of the CCCS delivered a systematic investment in the future generation of scholars, 'building and developing people for tomorrow'. In these ways, he was clearly an effective academic executive.[10]

In speaking of the palimpsest university, Barcan admits that while the demands of scholarly and corporate life are not the same, they can 'work in concert with each other' (Barcan 2013, p. 108). For a protracted time, Turner has been maestro of this concert. He conducted the art of management in such a way as to prove that administration was not a surrender to power but a creative process of channelling resources that can equip others to organize. If Turner's particular blend of the bureaucratic ethos with the deliverables of the executive worked well for his term as a research director, the question it raises for others is whether the same solutions will suit the university to come (Edu-Factory Collective 2009, Rogerro 2011). As a field, we are challenged by Graeme's legacy to work together to influence the terms of our own management, especially so that no one individual carries the responsibility for the field and its forward momentum. The model of service underpinning Turner's contribution produced an ironic counter-effect. As an institutional warrior, he mastered 'the rules of the game' for others' benefit. But the very success of Turner's advocacy, and the quiet determination he applied to mastering these techniques, protected many of his peers and subordinates from learning these same skills for themselves. Following Graeme, we must address this deficit and tackle management 'common sense' (Gramsci 1971) with all of the resources our disciplinary heritage provides. Ad hoc professionals turn to each other for support to withstand the turbulent conditions of work in the knowledge industries, to find methods for succeeding in spite of them. We may not all seek to be executives, but collectively we can be effective.

Disclosure statement

No potential conflict of interest was reported by the author.

Notes

1   A former Cultural Studies Department Chair offered this perspective in a discussion of this paper in earlier form. I would like to maintain confidentiality of the author as the comment appeared on a private social media page.
2   This paper draws on a more extensive account of management theory and the rise of productivity thinking to be published in Gregg (forthcoming).
3   For the purposes of this essay, I am limiting my account of Cultural Studies history to the tradition that Turner adopted and helpfully explained to so many students in his definitive overview text, *British Cultural Studies: An Introduction* (2002).
4   He was equally disdainful of the commercial mindset that threatened the quality of already existing degree programmes. His critique of digital media and creative industries courses in later writing (Turner 2012) came from the

basis that they were market-driven, erasing traditional values of Humanities education and threatening the civic purpose of the university.

5   Conscious of this split, in 2008 Graeme Turner, Mark Andrejevic and I offered a graduate course for UQ Masters and Ph.D. students combining our shared research interests. My own position at the CCCS from 2004–2006 was an exception to the typical three-year, research-only postdoc. Funding for my fellowship included a 25 percent share with the School of English, Media Studies and Art History, providing valuable lecturing, tutoring, convening and marking experience with undergraduates at various stages in their degree.

6   As a corporate researcher I often explain this as the major shift in perspective that a transition to industry work brings: the audience for your writing and communication typically narrows to the company, and by implication, the industry. Depending on the size of the company, this can mean a smaller or larger impact than university teaching and research.

7   The period I describe here, from 2009 to 2012, gave rise to a number of conversations about the experience of so-called casual or 'sessional' teachers in Australia, including the State of the Industry conference mentioned later in this article. This event was a collective effort with a team of colleagues – Clif Evers, Emily Potter, Fergus Grealy and Graeme Turner, among others – shepherding participation from 40 speakers across 20 universities nationwide. See Gregg (2009b). Following this event, public discussion of precarious academic work conditions and the consequences of online course offerings has been a feature of Australian blogs such as Music for Deckchairs (http://musicfordeckchairs.wordpress.com), the website of University of Wollongong academic Kate Bowles and landmark publications such as Whelan et al.'s (2013) *Zombies in the Academy: Living Death in Higher Education*.

8   This argument arises from helpful conversations with Mark Hayward.

9   Ien Ang, Tony Bennett, Stuart Cunningham, John Hartley, Ian Hunter, Elspeth Probyn, Krishna Sen and Mandy Thomas were just some of Turner's fellow travellers securing the institutional ground for Australian Cultural Studies research in the period I worked at the CCCS (2004–2008).

10 Of course, the executive world envisioned by Drucker and many of his contemporaries was a male-dominated domain with few female leaders. The challenge of creating a university work culture that values women as managers is something the present generation of Cultural Studies practitioners needs to overcome. It has not been pleasing to see so many inspiring female peers leave the University of Queensland in recent years for better working conditions. On women's experience as university managers, see Deem and Ozga (1997). On the proportion of Australian female academics in low-rung precarious academic employment as opposed to leadership positions, see Welch (2012).

References

Anderson, P. (1980) *Arguments within English Marxism*, London, Verso.

Barcan, R. (2013) *Academic Life and Labour in the New University: Hope and Other Choices*, London, Ashgate.

Bogost, I. (2013) 'Hyperemployment, or the exhausting work of the technology user', *The Atlantic*, 8 November, http://www.theatlantic.com/technology/archive/2013/11/hyperemployment-or-the-exhausting-work-of-the-technology-user/281149/ (accessed 18 June 2014).

Boltanski, L. & Chiapello, È. (2005) *The New Spirit of Capitalism*, trans. Gregory Elliott, New York, Verso.

Byron, J. (2015) 'Politics as scholarly practice: Graeme Turner and the art of advocacy', *Cultural Studies*. doi:10.1080/09502386.2014.1000607.

Crainer, S. & Dearlove, D. (1999) *Gravy Training: Inside the Business of Business Schools*, San Francisco, Jossey-Bass.

Deem, R. & Ozga, J. (1997) 'Women managing for diversity in a postmodern world', in *Feminist Critical Policy Analysis: A Perspective from Post-secondary Education*, ed. Catherine Marshall, London, Farmer, pp. 25–40.

Drucker, P. (1966) *The Effective Executive*, London, Pan.

Du Gay, P. (2000) *In Praise of Bureaucracy*, London, Sage.

Edu-Factory Collective (2009) *Towards a Global Autonomous University*, Brooklyn, Autonomedia.

Evans, M. (2004) *Killing Thinking: The Death of the Universities*, London, Continuum.

Fiske, J., Hodge, B. & Turner, G. (1987) *Myths of Oz: Reading Australian Popular Culture*, Sydney, Allen & Unwin.

Frow, J. (2006) 'An exchange on theory and cultural studies', *Cultural Studies Review*, vol. 12, no. 1, pp. 181–201.

Frow, J. & Morris, M., eds. (1993) 'Introduction', in *Australian Cultural Studies: A Reader*, St Leonards, NSW, Allen & Unwin.

Gallop, J. (2002) *Anecdotal Theory*, Durham, NC, Duke University Press.

Gill, R. (2009) 'Breaking the silence: the hidden injuries of the Neoliberal University', in *Secrecy and Silence in the Research Process: Feminist Reflections*, eds. R. Ryan-Flood & R. Gill, London, Routledge, pp. 228–244.

Gorz, A. (2010) *The Immaterial: Knowledge, Value and Capital*, trans. C. Turner, London, Seagull Books.

Gramsci, A. (1971) *Selections from the Prison Notebooks of Antonio Gramsci*, New York, International Publishers.

Gregg, M. (2009a) 'Learning to (love) labour: production cultures and the affective turn', *Journal Communication and Critical/Cultural Studies*, vol. 6, no. 2, pp. 209–214.

Gregg, M. (2009b) 'Why academia is no longer a smart choice', *New Matilda*, 24 November, https://newmatilda.com/2009/11/24/why-academia-no-longer-smart-choice (accessed 23 September 2014).

Gregg, M. (2011) *Work's Intimacy*, Cambridge and Malden, MA, Polity.

Gregg, M. (forthcoming) *Counterproductive: A Brief History of Time Management*, Durham, NC, Duke University Press.

Hoggart, R. (1957) *The Uses of Literacy: Aspects of Working-class Life with Special Reference to Publications and Entertainments*, Harmondsworth, Penguin.

Hoggart, R. (1978) *An Idea and Its Servants: UNESCO from within*, London, Chatto & Windus.

Huczynski, A. (2006) *Management Gurus*, rev. ed., London, Routledge.

Jencks, C. & Silver, N. (2013) *Adhocism: The Case for Improvisation*, Cambridge, MA, MIT Press. (Originally published by Doubleday, 1972).

Kanter, R. (1993) *Men and Women of the Corporation*, New York, Basic Books.

King, N. (2010) 'Interview with Professor Graeme Turner, University of Queensland, November 9, 2007', *Television & New Media*, vol. 11, no. 2, pp. 143–156.

Lee, R. E. (2003) *Life and Times of Cultural Studies: The Politics and Transformation of the Structures of Knowledge*, Durham, NC, Duke University Press.

McKay, K. & Brass, K. (2011) 'Hired hands: casualised technology and labour in the teaching of Cultural Studies', *Cultural Studies Review*, vol. 17, no. 2, pp. 140–164. http://epress.lib.uts.edu.au/journals/index.php/csrj/article/view/2004 (accessed 23 September 2014).

Morris, M. (2006) *Identity Anecdotes: Translation in Media Culture*, London, Sage.

Owen, S., ed. (2008) *Richard Hoggart and Cultural Studies*, Basingstoke, Palgrave Macmillan.

Readings, B. (1997) *The University in Ruins*, Boston, MA, Harvard University Press.

Rogerro, G. (2011) *The Production of Living Knowledge: The Crisis of the University and the Transformation of Labor in Europe and North America*, Philadelphia, PA, Temple University Press.

Ross, A. (2000) 'The mental labor problem', *Social Text 63*, vol. 18, no. 2, pp. 1–31.

Thompson, E. P. (1978) *The Poverty of Theory and Other Essays*, New York, Monthly Review Press.

Thrift, N. (2005) *Knowing Capitalism*, London, Sage.

Turner, G. (1986) *National Fictions: Literature, Film, and the Construction of Australian Narrative*, Sydney, Allen and Unwin.

Turner, G. (2002) *British Cultural Studies: An Introduction*, 3rd edn, London, Routledge.

Turner, G. (2009) 'Keynote address', in *The State of the Industry Conference*, UNSW, Sydney, 26–27 November.

Turner, G. (2012) *What's Become of Cultural Studies?* London, Sage.

Turner, G. & Tulloch, J., eds. (1990) *Australian Television: Programs, Pleasure, and Politics*, St Leonards, NSW, Allen & Unwin.

Welch, A. (2012) 'Academic salaries, massification and the rise of an underclass in Australia', in *Paying the Professoriate: A Critical Comparison of Compensation and Contracts*, eds. P. G. Altbach, L. Reisberg, M. Yudkevich, G. Androushchak, & I. F. Pacheco, New York, Routledge, pp. 61–71.

Whelan, A., Walker, R., & Moore, C., eds. (2013) *Zombies in the Academy: Living Death in Higher Education*, Chicago, IL, University of Chicago Press.

Graeme Turner

AFTERWORD

So ... what has become of Australian cultural studies?

It is in the nature of collections such as these that they are very much driven by what can be seen in the rear view mirror. These essays respond to my work in varied ways, some of them personally touching, but all of them interesting, insightful and greatly appreciated. Almost inevitably, they provoke some nostalgia for a period when Australian cultural studies was very much on the rise internationally: the first half of the 1990s, when the idea that there might be culturally specific formations of cultural studies had some novelty in the field, and when Australia was among the most distinctive of these local formations. Not everyone in cultural studies at the time, of course, took such a positive view of the Australian contribution. I remember one British review of my edited collection of Australian cultural and media studies, *Nation, Culture, Text* (Turner 1993) dismissing my 'triumphalist account' of Australian cultural studies in the introductory essay with what could only be described as a sneer. Looking back now, I would concede that this was indeed a triumphalist history – or as Toby Miller might more generously describe it, an exercise in 'gentle nationalism'. In my defence, I would also argue that it spoke of a time when cultural studies in Australia was indeed vibrant, when it was punching well above its weight in the international field of cultural studies, and when it had something distinctive to say. How likely is it, I wonder, that anyone would be tempted to write a similar account of the state of Australian cultural studies in the present conjuncture? With all this nostalgia in play, implicitly seeing that period as a golden age – a transitory or fleeting moment, as Toby describes it – is it the case that we are agreeing that Australian cultural studies is now in decline? In this short afterword, I want to present my personal view on the current condition of cultural studies in Australia; I might also start out by looking at the rear view mirror, but I hope, in the end, to focus on the road ahead.

The institutional configurations within which Australian cultural studies prospered during the 1990s and early 2000s have changed significantly over the last decade – as they have in most places where neoliberal higher education policies have begun to bite. Support for the humanities and social sciences within the higher education sector in Australia has become much more uncertain; the whole sector has become more instrumentally focused upon a professional training agenda; and the behaviour of the conservative government, which was elected in 2013, has clearly emboldened those members of the commentariat who might once have been slightly more restrained in their attacks on academic disciplines with a critical political agenda. After almost a decade of relative quiet on this front, academics in cultural and media studies are once again subject to moral panics in the media about the influence of what (*still!*) gets labelled as 'postmodernism' in our universities ('Postmodernism! Run! Run for your lives!'). So, the operational environment within our universities is a little more hostile now than it was a decade ago.

That said, this comes after a period in which cultural studies prospered more than most disciplines in the humanities and social sciences; it had no trouble attracting students and it became one of the most successful research fields. Furthermore, most of what I would point to as significant shifts in the condition of cultural studies in Australia today are as much the product of development within the field, as of changes in the policy or institutional environment. The key shifts I have in mind include the declining institutional presence of undergraduate teaching programmes in cultural studies, an interdisciplinary reframing of the cultural studies research agenda around 'cultural research', and a geopolitical reorientation of the Australian cultural studies view of the world as it turns away from its initial focus on the UK or Europe, and from the subsequent engagement with the USA, in order to now face more directly towards Asia.

There are fewer freestanding cultural studies teaching programmes in Australia now. As the system has become increasingly market-driven, humanities and social science faculties have become increasingly frantic in their search for degree labels that will attract the interest of high school graduates and their parents. By and large, those offering what look like the best prospects for employment have risen to the top. While there has never been a strong distinction between media and cultural studies in Australia, it is probably the case that media studies has begun to edge out cultural studies as the *de facto* disciplinary core for programmes in journalism and in media production programmes such as multimedia or television. New degree programmes in creative industries, new media studies, digital media and internet studies have appeared and have been relatively successful in representing themselves as skills-based programmes tailored to the employment market. Cultural studies has lost some of its fashionable cachet among undergraduates to these new programmes; the lure of digital media is an important factor here, but also the expansion of the higher education system over the last decade has resulted in patterns of student choices that appear to be more pragmatic and instrumentalist. That said, there are still large and highly successful undergraduate and graduate programmes in cultural studies that seem entirely secure within their institution and within the student market.

In research, cultural studies has maintained its high standing; it came in as one of the top five disciplines across the whole sector in the last national research assessment exercise, and it continues to secure high levels of funding for cultural studies research projects and fellowships. However, the research field of cultural studies in Australia has also changed significantly over this last decade. There has been the fragmentation I have addressed elsewhere (Turner 2011), with the surge of interest in digital media and the creative industries moving into some of the space formerly occupied by cultural studies. A more positive development, from my point of view, is the take-up of the label 'cultural research' which has effectively operated as a means of extending the purchase of cultural studies approaches. That label was initially attached to a government-funded, interdisciplinary research network that I convened between 2004 and 2011. (I should point out that I am not claiming the impact of this network as a personal achievement – it had 75 members, including most of those led Australian cultural studies at the time, and most who lead it now.) The ARC Cultural Research Network brought together researchers from a range of disciplines – including cultural geography, cultural anthropology, cultural history, and cultural studies – that shared an interest in culture as their central problematic. While it was cultural studies that provided the shared language which enabled conversations to occur, the network did not attempt to fold all these approaches back into cultural studies. Rather, it set a varied and broadly based interdisciplinary agenda of topics and methodologies for cultural studies-informed research. Through its development of this agenda, cultural studies, for many who work in the humanities and the social sciences now, has played an enabling interdisciplinary role – bringing people and approaches together around common interests and objectives. The result, perhaps, is a slight dilution of the cultural studies project, but this is balanced, in my view, against the benefits that come from the extension of its purchase and its intellectual reach – something I experienced personally myself in my collaboration with Anna Cristina Pertierra (Pertierra and Turner 2013). While this development has occurred, cultural studies' hard-won reputation as a leading field of research and enquiry has remained intact, and along the way, the amount of collaborative cross-disciplinary research in the broad field of cultural and media studies has expanded dramatically.

What is most interesting about this latter development, is where it is occurring. While there has been a lot of cultural research on Australian subjects, involving collaboration in particular between cultural geographers, cultural historians and cultural studies researchers, the last decade has seen an increasing engagement with researchers in Asia. An example would be the forthcoming book, *Telemodernities*, on lifestyle television and modernity in Asia, written by Tania Lewis, Fran Martin and Wanning Sun – who have records of collaborative work in India, Taiwan and China, respectively. Teams of researchers based in Australia connecting with researchers in Asia, which is turning into a powerhouse of cultural studies activity, are becoming relatively common. Stuart Cunningham's research centre at QUT was one of the earliest proponents of this sort of organized intellectual exchange through, in particular, the efforts of Michael Keane. Also, there has been the significant ripple effect from Meaghan Morris's 12 years as professor of cultural studies at Lingnan University in Hong Kong. Meaghan's work there brought quite a number of Australians, including myself, into much more direct and productive engagement with Asian cultural studies researchers than had occurred before. In my case, it was my involvement with Meaghan's staff and students which led to the development of an Asian strand in a large television project I led over 2006–2011 and which has resulted in two books published in collaboration with Jinna Tay (Turner and Tay 2009, Tay and Turner 2015). Australian cultural studies, in general, now seems more interested in engaging with, and researching in, Asia than Europe or the USA. That is a major change for a field which was initially, overwhelmingly, oriented towards French critical theory or British cultural studies and was dutifully observant of, if not entirely convinced about, American cultural studies ('not political enough' was the standard complaint). Mind you, as a warning to the limits of generalizations, Tony Bennett's contribution to this collection makes a distinctive argument for the revisiting of a major tradition of American anthropology as we revise the prehistories of cultural studies. That said, the diverse national and regional contexts in Asia that have fed into the InterAsia project are emerging as exciting testing grounds for the application of cultural studies ideas, raising new challenges for theory and for research. Australian cultural studies seems to be embracing those challenges enthusiastically.

On the downside of this, it may well be true, as Frances Bonner argues in her essay in this issue, that the increased commitment to engaging with international researchers has tended to leave some important Australian issues unexamined. That tension has been around for quite some time, as a direct consequence of Australian-based researchers achieving some international prominence and shifting their attention towards international or transnational debates. It is also the case that the motivations Toby Miller describes as cultural nationalism have declined in relevance for Australian cultural studies; I doubt whether many of the current generation of early career researchers would orient their work in that way with anything like the intensity that I did. Perhaps it is simply no longer necessary, and that battle has been won: contemporary Australian cultural studies seems uncomplicatedly confident of its status, and disinterested in imagining itself as a colonial formation. Nonetheless, vestiges of the cultural nationalist impulse survive in what has now become a standard, indeed possibly constitutive, ethico-political orientation for the field in Australia – the routine insistence on the specificity of its location, and on the strategic centrality of historicizing and properly contextualizing cultural studies research wherever it occurs.

If this, then, is what Australian cultural studies has become, its future as a field of research – particularly, in its engagement with Asia – looks at least as exciting, and certainly as distinctive, as what has gone before. On the one hand, Meaghan Morris's wonderful contribution to this collection demonstrates that there are still rich and effective ways of performing the located-ness of Australian cultural studies and, on the other hand, there is a new generation of rising stars who are highly active in international debates – particularly around new media, digital media and mobile media. Australian researchers have become more regular presences in the big international conferences as a consequence of their success in securing funding, and as a result of the development of a small number of research centres in the field which take the dissemination of their research extremely seriously. The institutional stability of cultural studies teaching programmes and research centres is less secure as it is much more dependent not only upon government policy and funding settings, but also upon the politics of funding within individual institutions. As John Byron's essay in this volume indicates, the task of maintaining the gains made within a changing policy environment is not for the faint-hearted, while the task of managing the politics of a cultural studies' presence within particular institutions involves some skills that cultural studies cannot be guaranteed to provide. Melissa Gregg makes the point, in her essay, that finding ways to build successful units within these institutions, even once funding has been secured, is also a daunting task involving not only academic, but also management, skills. There remains a great deal of potential, however, in cultural studies as a teaching programme in the present conjuncture. Some danger, I admit, lies in what has become a worrying trend towards the casualization of the academic workforce across the sector in Australia, and particularly in the humanities disciplines. If that trend continues or, worse, accelerates, it will suck the life out of our field of study, but the problem is becoming more widely recognized as one that needs to be addressed. In terms of the content and approach of our teaching programmes, as I have argued in *What's Become of Cultural Studies?* (Turner 2012), there is a lot that can be done to return the teaching of cultural studies in undergraduate programmes to the levels of excitement it generated initially – in Australia, and elsewhere. If that challenge is taken up, and if universities do provide genuine and continuing employment opportunities for this next generation of cultural studies teachers and scholars, there is reason to expect more from the undergraduate teaching programmes in cultural studies in Australia.

Let me conclude by thanking all of the contributors to this special issue for their generosity, for the quality of their contributions, and for their friendship over what is, in some cases, a great many years. I also would like to thank the stellar quartet of my former CCCS colleagues: Gerard Goggin, who conceived the project, and Anna Cristina Pertierra, Mark Andrejevic and Melissa Gregg, who shared the editorial tasks in bringing the idea to fruition. It is a wonderful thing you have given me. And, finally, let me thank another of my old friends, Larry Grossberg, for devoting an issue of this great journal to this purpose; I am truly grateful.

Disclosure statement

No potential conflict of interest was reported by the author.

References

Pertierra, A.C. & Turner, G. (2013) *Locating Television: Zones of Consumption*, London, Routledge.

Tay, J. & Turner, G. eds. (2015) *Television Histories in Asia*, London, Routledge.

Turner, G. ed. (1993) *Nation, Culture, Text: Australian Cultural and Media Studies*, London, Routledge.

Turner, G. (2011) 'Surrendering the space: convergence culture, cultural studies and the curriculum', *Cultural Studies*, vol. 25, no. 4–5, pp. 685–699.

Turner, G. (2012) *What's Become of Cultural Studies*, London, Sage.

Turner, G. & Tay, J. eds. (2009) *Television Studies after TV: Understanding Television in the Post-broadcast Era*, London and New York, NY, Routledge.

Index

www.ingramcontent.com/pod-product-compliance
Ingram Content Group UK Ltd.
Pitfield, Milton Keynes, MK11 3LW, UK
UKHW020348010325
455677UK00021B/344